Exploring Traditions –

Celebrating the Grange Way of Life

Walter Boomsma

Exploring Traditions — Celebrating the Grange Way of Life
by Walter Boomsma

Published by
Abbot Village Press
17 River Road
Abbot ME 04406

First Edition September 2018

Cover photo by Walter Boomsma

This is a work of nonfiction. No names have been changed, no characters invented, no events have been fabricated. The information in this book is true and complete to the best of our knowledge. All recommendations are made without guarantee on the part of the author or Abbot Village Press. The author and publisher disclaim any liability in connection with the use of this information.

Printed in the United States of America

ISBN -13: 978-1725905375

ISBN-10: 1725905375

Table of Contents

Foreward

The Grange Manual is full of beautiful language that could be studied as literature, using expressive words that we don't commonly use and may not clearly understand today. While it has been amended several dozen times, the meaning and most of the original words written 150 years ago remain the same, and as you read it, you will see the language and themes are even older still. Many of the ideas and much of the symbolism came from ancient writings of the Eleusinian Mysteries, a group that existed before the birth of Christ. The first sentence of the officers' Installation Ceremony states, "Since God placed man on Earth, agriculture has existed." Agriculture began in the Garden of Eden and still sustains life on Earth today, so lessons drawn from the soil are indeed timeless.

The lessons taught in the four degrees, the initiation ceremonies to join a local Grange, were based on farm life and as such were clear and recognizable to those who became members, because in our beginning years, to be a Granger you must have been part of a farm family. These lessons hold just as true today but may not be as easily understood by people who are now three or four generations removed from the farm. The language may seem archaic to the modern ear and require study of the written words, as we study Shakespeare or ancient literature.

These essays by Walter Boomsma unpack the teachings of the Grange and relate them to today's world and our everyday lives. He has a gift for taking the lessons from the farm and showing their relevance today, even for those whose only interaction with agriculture happens through their food and clothing choices. He understands the meaning the Grange Founders intended and interprets the sometimes archaic language to reveal the principles they wanted to teach to farm families who often had no other opportunity for education.

In this 150th year of the Order of Patrons of Husbandry, it is important that Grange members as well as people who have never heard of the Grange but have benefited from its influence come to understand the great history, traditions, and the Ritual that have sustained the organization through these many years and through amazing changes in society, agriculture, industry, and government. Walter's writings show clearly that the Grange remains relevant in the modern era and can still assist its members in facing the challenges of life in the modern world.

Betsy E. Huber
Master (President)
The National Grange
Washington D.C.

Preface

When I first wrote the preface to *Small People—Big Brains* in 2013 I expressed hope that someday someone would do a study of how many people read the preface of books. As far as I know, that study still hasn't been done. I do hope you're reading this one.

For those who might not know, the purpose of a preface is to provide "an explanation or defense" of how the book came about.

To understand the beginning of this book requires at least a brief explanation of the Grange, an organization with a 150-year history replete with tradition and ritual. When I joined the Grange, I found much of that tradition and ritual to be a bit mysterious—the Grange does have a reputation for being a "secret society." The reasons for that reputation are found in its history and teachings. But it is far less secret today than often thought.

Unfortunately, as so often happens, the reasons and explanations for some of its rituals and traditions get lost to habit and practice.

When I became the Communications Director for the Maine State Grange, I developed even more interest in how what we practice (do) communicates. Many a parent has said, "Do as I say, not as I do," leaving their child confused. It may have been a child who coined the observation, "What you are doing is shouting so loudly I can't hear what you are saying."

I remembered as a new Granger how many times I was told to do or not do something but without any explanation. "Do as we do." Being a curious person by nature, I found myself hungering for explanations of "the Grange way of life." The irony I discovered is that the Grange truly values education, thinking and growth. While I don't pretend to be an expert, I have learned a lot about Grange traditions and ritual.

As Communications Director, I decided there would be value in sharing what I was learning and, in some cases, challenging members' knowledge of what we often routinely practice. A monthly column for our website and printed bulletin would do just that. We would explore traditions and meander around the Grange Way of Life.

After three years of columns, the logical next step was to collect them into book form and you now hold the result in your hand. The fact that the Grange is still around after 150 years supports the idea that the teachings of the Grange are timeless.

This is not offered as a "Guide to the Grange" nor does it purport to define Grange practice and thinking. It's quite the contrary. The key word in the title is "Explore." One of the things I particularly value about my Grange membership is that it is a constant source of challenge and truly "makes me think."

That, my friend, is my hope for you as you explore, that you will think and develop a deeper understanding of and appreciation for this organization called "the Grange."

Acknowledgments

Any degree or Ritual quotations are from the forty-sixth edition of the 2013 Subordinate Grange Manual and the current Pomona Grange Manual and are shown in *italic print.*

The views and opinions expressed in "Exploring Traditions" are those of the author and do not necessarily reflect the official doctrine and policy of the Grange.

I am indebted to my Grange Brothers and Sisters who generously shared their understanding of Grange Ritual and practice. I am perhaps even more indebted to Grange Brothers and Sisters who have been curious and asked questions.

A special thanks goes to Betsy Huber, National Grange Master, and Amanda Brozana Rio, National Grange Communications Director for their support and encouragement of both my column and this book..

Thanks also to my wife, Janice, for being my Grange Partner and proofreader. A major factor in our decision to join the Grange was that it was something we could do together, so it's especially appropriate that she is part of this book!

The Beautiful Lessons We Learn in the Grange

Our season of work in the Grange now has passed
With lessons of life that we all should hold fast;
The home and the farm and each change of the year,
The beauty of landscape, all make us we revere
The wonderful lessons we learn in the Grange.

In springtime while working in household and field
The virtue of faithfulness stands forth revealed;
In summer the value of order discern,
And habits of industry grow as we learn.
The beautiful truths that are taught in the Grange.

In autumn we're joyous and freely confess
The bounty of Him who we gratefully bless;
In winter we've leisure for culture and rest,
And in the home circle we gladly attest
The wonderful lessons we learn in the Grange.

Let's cherish our ritual and keep it alive,
Plan wisely the future and earnestly strive
With charity, hope and faith from on High
To try with fidelity now to apply
The beautiful lessons we learn in the Grange

(The Grange Songbook, 1983)
Words by Alfred Vivian, © 1930, Ohio State Grange

Dedication

To Betty Van Dyke, Granger Extraordinaire!

As a senior member of Valley Grange when I first joined Betty was a huge influence during my "formative years" as a Patron of Husbandry. I came to appreciate both her knowledge of the Grange teachings and her commitment to what later I understood to be the Grange Way of Life. Anyone who knows Betty will understand that we didn't always agree, but Betty truly practices the Grange Motto, a summary of the Grange way of life:

In essentials, unity; in non-essentials, liberty. In all things, charity.

Exploring Traditions –
Celebrating the Grange Way of Life

The Harvest Season

We are well into the harvest season; the season of the Third Degree. In the Third Degree candidates strive to become harvesters and gleaners. The term gleaner is not commonly used today, but it historically refers to those who follow those who reap and harvest, collecting (gleaning) that which is left behind. The word connotes a slow and deliberate approach.

If we listen carefully to the words of the degree, there is a great deal of logic to the fact that this degree of harvest includes the lesson of charity. Charity is about benevolence and is often considered synonymous with love. Many are familiar with the concept of sowing and reaping, heeding the caution that "whatsoever ye sow, that also shall ye reap." I recall a slightly more humorous outlook that if one is going to "sow wild oats on the weekend" it might be best to "pray for a crop failure on Monday."

Ripley Farm in Dover Foxcroft recently announced a Community Carrot Harvest. A large bed of carrots was planted last spring with the full intention those carrots be harvested and donated to the local food cupboards. Harvesters and gleaners are being sought and the entire event reminds me of the Chaplain's observation during the instruction, "Be faithful in gathering, that you may be liberal in dispensing."

The master of the Fourth Degree explains the emblem of the Fourth Degree, the sickle. *"…It speaks of peace and prosperity, and is the harbinger of joy. It is used not merely to reap the golden grain for the sheaf, but, in the field of mind and heart and soul, to gather every stalk, every opening flower, every desirable fruit. Thus shall the implement prove a reminder of honorable employment, preaching its sermon of present prosperity and peace, and its prophecy of future plenty and rejoicing."*

I remember during my childhood how entire families were invited into potato fields after the harvest to glean what we could use. It was hard work but also included some camaraderie as we took to the fields. Some families were able to lay up a season's worth of potatoes in the root cellar just for the picking. It was an honorable employment.

As Grangers, we are challenged to harvest and glean not only produce for the body, also those things for the "mind and heart and soul." And, as if that is not a big enough challenge, we are also instructed to "be liberal in dispensing."

Flora concludes the lesson with the charge, *"…dispense charity, the flower of brotherly love, as freely as Nature spreads her flowery carpet over all the earth. And let your charity extend to all humanity."*

As we travel through the field of life, there are plenty of opportunities to harvest and perhaps even more to glean. The challenges of the Fourth Degree are not easy. But as the Overseer reminds us, *"Cultivate the habit of looking for better and brighter days, instead of mourning over the past… When you strive to make labor honoruble, exert yourself to make it pleasant and cheerful for all around you."*

If you call my cell phone and I'm not available, you'll hear this message: "Sorry I can't take your call right now. I'm out trying to make the world a better and happier place." The world is a big place and there are times when the challenge of making it better and happier seems overwhelming. But the one thing we all have to dispense is charity. Grangers should be dispensing it liberally.

What Tool Shall We Use?

"The spade we use when we wish to penetrate deeper into the soil than we can with the plow. It thus becomes the emblem of thoroughness. Whatsover you attempt to do, strive to do it well." These are the words spoken by the master to the candidates during the First Degree, the degree of preparation. The master is, of course, describing the implements of the first degree—the ax, plow, harrow, and spade.

Each implement serves a different purpose when working the soil. And each implement represents a different application to what might be considered the Grange Way of Life.

The ax is *"used to cut away obstructions…"* and as we think about the repeated blows sometimes necessary to cut through the hardest wood we are reminded that *"repeated trials surmount every difficulty."*

The plow is used to *"break up the ground…"* and might represent how we *"prepare the mind for growth…"* by plowing through the *"heavy soil of ignorance."*

The harrow pulverizes the soil and covers the seed. In the instruction, the master suggests this is *"emblematic of that course of study and observation necessary for you fully to understand…"*

And the spade is used to *"penetrate deeper,"* suggesting the need for thoroughness. These implements are not just about the soil; they are about our minds and our work.

Grange language can be most interesting. When degrees are discussed there seems to be some diversity of vocabulary. We sometimes ask, "Have you received the degrees?" But I've also heard "Have you taken the degrees?" Less frequently the question is, "Have you been through the degrees?"

As a writer, I think words are important—including how we describe the degrees. If we turn to the degrees themselves, the most frequent word used to describe them is "instructed." (Just prior to the portion of the first degree referred to here, the assistant steward says to the master, *"…our brothers and sisters are prepared to receive your instruction."*) The degrees are not meant to be a passive activity. As candidates, we are instructed and we learn. Is it odd that we don't say, "I've learned the degrees?"

The master's use of these implements is very instructive and includes a lesson we should learn. When faced with life's challenges, is it not logical that we might best begin by remembering that sometimes we need determination and a desire to keep trying. And early on we need to do some research, get some facts, and "plow through" our own ignorance. When we do so, we shouldn't just skim the surface. Our goal should be to fully understand. So much so that we grab our spades and dig deep, making sure we are thorough in our quest.

Here's an idea that might take a while to catch on… during our meetings when we discuss an idea or a problem, could someone suggest we use the implements of the First Degree during our discussion? Should we be using an ax, plow, harrow, or spade? All four are necessary. All four contribute.

Maybe a member will call out, "Hey! I've been instructed in the First Degree! I think we should use a spade here. Let's make sure we're being thorough and do this well!"

And perhaps before the meeting is over we'll remember the Lecturer's instruction, *"…while occupied in the work of preparing your lands for the seed, have faith in God's promise that seedtime and harvest shall never fail…"*

Moving Forward; Moving Backward

"It is now the Fourth Degree, in the Grange, on the farm, and in our lives… In winter, the season of rest from active toil, we sit down with our families, our friends and neighbors, and enjoy together the good things our labors in the lower degrees have brought us. So also in old age we enjoy the fruits of a well-spent life, surrounded by friends, and in a happy home."

The Steward encourages the candidates to remember that *"it is in the home that we enjoy the fruits of our labors in the fields of the farm and the fields of life."* For those of us who live in Maine, winter does seem to encourage us to spend more time in our homes. Our modern technology and conveniences may, however, mean that we spend less time "enjoying the fruits of a well-spent life" and more time watching television or using our i-Pad to check social media sites.

The Fourth Degree is perhaps a degree of reflection. When I read the above passage, my eyes and mind focused on the phrase "old age" and for some reason, I connected it to this quote I recently used in a presentation:

"One curious thing about growing up is that you don't only move forward in time; you move backward as well, as pieces of your parents' and grandparents' lives come to you and stay with you."

Life **is** about movement and there are interesting parallels as we move through the degrees—with life and the seasons of the year. Most Grangers know that each degree represents a season and the degrees themselves are progressive. In an interesting way, one of the continued challenges for our organization often centers around the word "progress."

While I'm far from an expert, I'm "working my way

through the degrees" as part of these ongoing columns. If you haven't tried it, I can assure you that curling up with a Grange Manual on a cold winter night can be a very relaxing and rewarding experience.

As I move through the manual, I can find nothing that bans progress and change—quite the contrary, actually. I also find nothing that requires us to abandon the past. But I do see much about growth and movement. Even in this passage, we are encouraged to enjoy the fruits of our labors both in the fields of the farm and fields of life.

One curious thing about the life of our Grange is that we aren't just moving forward in time; we are moving backward as well, as pieces of our past come to us and stay with us.

The Fourth Degree is also about fidelity and friendship. It contains one of my favorite teachings. The Overseer tells the candidates to *"…look with earnest solicitude upon children and their welfare; and remember that they are to follow in our footsteps and occupy our positions. If we desire to encourage them to love rural life, we must make its labors cheerful. What a child sees makes the most lasting impression. We may tell them of the pleasures and independence of the farmer's life; but if their daily intercourse with us shows it to be tedious, irksome, laborious, without any recreation of body or mind, they will soon lose all interest in it and seek employment elsewhere…"*

Application of Grange teaching has a wondrous aspect in that the lessons can be applied in so many different ways. I challenge you to reread the Overseer's lesson and change the word "children" to "others" and the words "rural" and "farmer" to "Grange" and "Granger." It would sound like this:

"...look with earnest solicitude upon others and their welfare; and remember that they are to follow in our footsteps and occupy our positions. If we desire to encourage them to love Grange life, we must make its labors cheerful. What another sees makes the most lasting impression. We may tell them of the pleasures and independence of the Granger's life; but if their daily intercourse with us shows it to be tedious, irksome, laborious, without any recreation of body or mind, they will soon lose all interest in it and seek membership and friendship elsewhere..."

Bye, Bye, Longjohns!

An article in the Maine Policy Review* serves both as a reminder of the importance of music in Grange Tradition and an interesting bit of Maine Trivia. The article is entitled "The Digital Humanities Imperative" and discusses the digital preservation of Maine Folklore and Oral History. Interesting as the article is, the sidebar example is what caught my eye.

The example is a song written in Maine during the late twentieth century. It began as one verse written, "by the nephew of Grange member Myrtle McKinney, who was also the official musician in Norridgewock, ME." It is believed the song had multiple authors including Dottie Abbott, a resident of the Forks and member of Bingham Grange.

Sung to the tune of "Bye-Bye Blackbird," there can be little doubt the song was sung as a closing song in the in the early spring. The first verse is:

I put them on October one, that was orders from my hon,
How long, longjohns?
They'll keep me warm all winter, long, I want to tell you in this song,
How long, longjohns?
They were closer to me than a friend, next year to Sears again I'll send;
I kind of miss this underwear, for several months we were a pair,
Longjohns, bye-bye!

And the third verse completes the story:

I'd have shed my underwear, I don't care, I'll go bare.
Bye-bye, longjohns!
There were very close to me, they tickled me, tee hee hee,
Bye-bye, longjohns.

If you see them you'll know where to find me;
I have shed my underwear but I don't care, I'll go bare.
Longjohns, bye-bye!

While we may say goodbye to our longjohns, fortunately, we do not say goodbye to the music of an earlier time. Why not give this one a try at your next meeting? Music has always played an important role in our meetings and activities. Let the tradition continue!

Maine Policy Review, Vol. 24, No.1, 2015, published by the Margaret Chase Institute.

A Granger's Daily Life

It might be seen as unfortunate that we most often only install officers once a year for there is much to consider in the installing officer's opening remarks. We learn, for example, that our Order's teachings, *"…accompany members in their daily pursuits. They form part of the farmer's daily life. They do not call him from his work to put his mind on any other subject, but furnish recreation in his daily duties, and by cheerful instruction, lighten and elevate his labor."*

I am always a little saddened when I hear comments like "our Grange doesn't meet in the winter," in part because it feels somehow wrong—as if we are setting aside what is meant to be an important part of our daily life. I do understand the practicalities of sub-zero temperatures and winter travel difficulties. But I also wonder how many meetings our forefathers canceled because of weather.

I have often said that I don't think our forefathers founded the Grange so we could have meetings and "do" the Ritual. Those activities are clearly secondary and designed to support what the Grange is supposed to be doing. I started this series of columns in a large part because I wanted to learn what the "Grange way of life" is all about. How does being a Granger impact our lives and "lighten and elevate" our labor?

We are an organization driven by teaching whether it be in degree work, the Obligation Ceremony, or Installation of Officers. Our meeting Ritual is designed to remind us of those teachings and every meeting includes a "lecturer's program" that should be stimulating our thinking. All this teaching at least implies just what role the Grange should play in our daily lives. *"Honesty is inculcated, education nurtured, temperance supported, brotherly love captivated, and charity made an essential characteristic."* The installing officer is, it seems, reminding us of what the Grange is all about. There is, of course, an emphasis on agriculture both as a science and as a way to *"enhance the value and increase the attractions of our home."*

Valley Grange Master Jim Annis is fond of observing, "You rarely see a skinny Granger." Perhaps we are paying too much heed to the first part of the installing officer's reminder, *"…we believe there is nothing better for a man than that he should eat and drink and he should make his soul enjoy good in his labor."*

Duties and responsibilities accompany Grange membership, but it must not escape our notice that words like "cheerful" and "enjoy" appear often in the installing officer's comments and throughout Grange teaching. When we begin to fully understand those teachings, we discover that Grange life is about far more than meetings and the Ritual. *"… to all interested in Agriculture, who have generous hearts and open hands to help the needy, raise the fallen, and aid in making the labors of this life cheerful, we say, 'Welcome to the Grange.'"*

If you call my cell phone number and I don't answer, you'll get to hear me say, "Sorry I can't take your call right now. I'm busy trying to make the world a better and happier place." When I first adopted it, I was just trying to do something different and perhaps a little entertaining. It's now become both a personal mission and a slogan. When you think of it, isn't that what a Granger should be doing? Maybe the next time somebody asks me what the Grange does I'll answer, "We make the world a better and happier place." It could be just that simple.

Whose Motto Is It?

For several years now, our annual vacation has included a visit to central Pennsylvania where we spend some time among "the plain people" (Amish, Mennonites, Hutterites). As a society, they have some very parallel considerations to fraternal organizations such as the Grange. I was particularly interested in the fact that many Amish (particularly Old Order, the most conservative) do not have an understanding of the English need for "why." In a way that we might find fatalistic if you ask them "Why do you…" they almost do not understand the question. "We just do… it just is…"

While this might seem illogical to "outsiders," this acceptance no doubt contributes to their peaceful and serene way of life. We tend to need and want understanding. Or do we?

If we took an aspect of the Ritual and asked a Granger "Why do you…" (not cross between the altar and the Graces, for example) how many would have an answer and what that answer would be? I honestly do not know the answer and, admittedly, haven't been curious enough to research it.

But I stumbled on to something during one of those Pennsylvania visits that did get me curious. We were traveling through Lititz when I stopped for a photo opportunity on the grounds of the Moravian Church. Imagine my surprise when I learned the Moravian Church's motto or slogan:

In essentials unity, in non-essentials liberty, and in all things love.

I confess. My instinctive response was that they'd "borrowed" this from the Grange, changing the word charity to love. Research proved that wrong. While I was unable to learn when the Grange first claimed it as a slogan, I did learn that the earliest references date back to the 1600's and attribute it to Augustine of Hippo, a church father from the fifth century. The Moravians themselves admit it is used by several other religious groups and it was probably "claimed" by the Moravian Church in the early 1900's.

History aside, it's a pretty good motto, not only for our order but for our daily lives.

In essentials, unity… We are a diverse organization and society—that's both a blessing and a curse. By its very nature, diversity creates conflict that requires management. Can we answer the question of "What are the essentials?" There is evidence that the original purpose of this three-part quote was to encourage theologians to develop greater unity by focusing on essentials.

In non-essentials, liberty… One way we manage potential conflict is to allow freedom (liberty) on the "non-essentials." We are encouraged to allow our brothers and sisters liberty to believe and pursue those ends we may not agree on. I learned this lesson from my oldest daughter when she was two years old. We were visiting the coast and she kept excitingly pointing and exclaiming, "Birds, Daddy! Birds!" Each time I would gently correct her, "Those are seagulls, Bethanie." After having the conversation several times, she somewhat exasperatedly said, "You call 'em seagulls. I'll call 'em birds." In non-essentials, liberty, thank you.

In all things. charity… My curious mind wonders if the word choice here was deliberate. Why do we use the word "charity" and the Moravians use "love?" Admittedly, those words are seen as synonymous in many religious circles, but there does seem to be a connotative difference. It is also of interest that some versions of this motto make this third point a bit differently:

In essentials unity, in non-essentials, liberty, and in both things, love.

or

Unity in necessary things, freedom in unnecessary things, and in both things, love.

One of the reasons people flock to "Amish Country" is a fascination with what is perceived as unity and peace and a sense of community that works. Most tourists like brushing up against it, but they don't take the time to understand it and they are far from willing to adopt the practices necessary to create it. I have long believed our Order could not only succeed but could prosper if we could simply figure out how to offer a similar sense of community to a society that needs and wants it. Perhaps the answer lies in "our" motto.

Read some of the history of this motto in the Moravian Archives:

http://www.moravianchurcharchives.org/thismonth/12_05%20I n%20Essentials.pdf

Symbolism Should Not Lose Meaning

In last month's column, I admitted ignorance of one aspect of Grange Ritual. "Why do we not cross between the altar and the graces?" I even admitted to not being curious enough to research it. They say, "Confession is good for the soul," but I'm also going to report that no one offered to enlighten me. For the past month, I've been left wonder if, perhaps, I am not alone in my ignorance.

That somewhat makes the point that it is quite easy for symbolism to lose its meaning. In the opening charge prior to conferral of the First Degree the master reminds us, *The underlying philosophy of the Grange is portrayed by the oldest and most successful method of communication known to man – the use of symbols.*

Not to embarrass myself or anyone else, I'm obligated to point out that the answer to the question is actually found in the First Degree instruction. In his charge, the master also says that *"…symbolism will be fully explained at the appropriate time."* I suppose I could suggest that I wasn't paying attention—not only when I was instructed, but also during the many times I have participated in or observed the First Degree. My explanation (or excuse) is that a lot happens during those first four degrees. No matter how many times you hear and see them it's easy to be overwhelmed. Hearing or saying the words is no guarantee that all of the lessons will be truly understood and internalized.

One of the real joys I've experienced from writing this monthly column is being able to take some time to read and ponder the many lessons contained in the the Ritual. Sometimes I will stop after as little as a paragraph, close the book, and consider what can be learned. A second reading will provide the continuity and often give a "bigger picture." Most Grangers do recognize that our organization was ahead of its time by the equal standing it gave women. That's the big picture. In fact, in the First Degree, the Lecturer states, *"Therefore, remember the high position assigned to womanhood, and sustain it with dignity and grace."*

Soon after, the candidates are conducted to the master. After providing the "secret instructions," the master of the First Degree clearly explains, *"It is also my duty to instruct you that to honor womanhood and show reverence for the Bible we respectively refrain from passing between the Altar and the station of the Graces when the Grange is in session, except as prescribed in the manual."*

So now you know! I know I was not the only ignorant person on this point, for I have asked the question more than once and had others admit they didn't know either. Perhaps it's time for a campaign on this point. During our next meeting, might we raise this lesson, perhaps as a "suggestion for the good of the Order?" Feel free to use this column. It will only take a few minutes to read it.

For that matter, another suggestion for the good of the Order might be to make it a practice to have someone read one selected paragraph from the degree work just prior to the close of every meeting. It just might help us *"Add dignity to our labor, and in our dealings with our fellow men be honest, be just, and fear not."*

The Staves Remind Us

One of the honors bestowed upon me as lecturer/program director for Valley Grange is conducting the annual "Dictionary Day" for schools and classes receiving dictionaries. We currently have two districts making field trips to the Grange Hall and we have a team that visits two other districts.

In talking about the Grange, I use and explain the staves to the kids as a way of talking about the importance of tools. The kids are always fascinated by the staves and what they represent. Many times they draw the staves on their thank you notes. (The owl seems to be a frequent favorite.) I'm always impressed that they can remember all four!

The spud is, of course, the emblem of the Steward and is an "ancient implement" used by Stewards to eliminate roots or weeds from the fields. In the Installation Ceremony, it becomes clear that it serves to remind the steward of his/her duty to *"prevent or remove all causes of disagreement in the Grange and our Order."*

The Assistant Stewards carry the pruning hook as an emblem of peace (since it is created from a spear) and a shepherd's crook as a reminder "s*o should you nurture your members."*

The owl carried by the Gatekeeper deserves some attention. In the early days of the Grange, the Gatekeeper was, in every sense of the word, "on guard" and positioned between the outer and inner gates to prevent entry of unauthorized persons. We should remember that this was done to protect the "secret work" of the Grange which was, simply stated, to advance the farmer in a time when other groups were often exploiting farmers. The Grange provided an opportunity to strategize literally behind closed doors.

In the 2013 Subordinate Grange Manual, there is an "Alternative Installation Ceremony" that adds a new dimension to the Gatekeeper's duties, more accurately representing how the Grange does its work today. *"...be vigilant and watchful... you are the first contact with visitors and guests. Be sure to introduce them to members and be courteous and friendly to all."* Some have even suggested the position of "Gatekeeper" should be changed to "Greeter."

In the few minutes we have with the kids, it's fun to consider the lessons of the staves. The Grange is an organization where we try to manage disagreement—remember our motto? ***In essentials, unity. In nonessentials, liberty. In all things, charity.*** Peace should naturally follow and, while we labor to serve our communities, we ought not to forget to nurture ourselves, in part by pruning away discord.

As an organization steeped in tradition and ritual, we should value that—but not to the extent we stop being courteous and friendly to all. When we look at the big picture, the Grange is not meant to be a "can't" organization. It was meant to be a "can" organization, powerful in its unity of purpose. Consider the master's reminders as we close our meetings. *"Let us not forget the principles of our order. Let us add dignity to labor and in our dealings with our fellow men, be honest, be just, and fear not. We must avoid intemperance in eating, drinking, and language, also in work and recreation, and whatever we do, strive to do it well..."*

What Do Grangers Stand For?

What does the Grange stand for? Or perhaps a more interesting question would be "What do people _think_ the Grange stands for?"

We can refer to our Declaration of Principles for an answer. While this is a noble task (and might be the basis for a lecturer's program), we'll get an official but somewhat conceptual understanding. I wanted something more basic and down to earth. Therefore, I decided to step outside the Grange Circle.

One perception I encountered seemed simplistic and to the point. It suggested that the Grange is "a fraternal organization… that encourages families to band together to promote the economic and political well-being of the community and agriculture." There's a lot to like in that definition.

As with any organization that has a long history, there's the opportunity for some blending of the past and present. Another description I encountered focused more on the historical outlook suggesting the Grange was founded "to advance methods of agriculture, as well as to promote the social and economic needs of farmers."

Turning again to an official source, the preamble to the National Grange Constitution explains, "The ultimate object of this organization is for mutual instruction and protection, to lighten labor by diffusing a knowledge of its aims and purposes, to expand the mind by tracing the beautiful laws the Great Creator has established in the Universe, and to enlarge our views of creative wisdom and power."

I'll never forget one call I got from a client during my consulting career. He'd been to a conference over the weekend on the topic of creating organizational excellence. He called me Monday morning and said,

"I'm really fired up and motivated. I want to make this organization into something great. But I'm sitting here at my desk and I don't know what to do or where to start!"

So the pressing question might be how we take these somewhat lofty purposes and give them meaning in our daily lives. If we can't translate those purposes into practice, we may find ourselves no longer relevant. It's practice that gives purpose meaning.

To use an agricultural metaphor, we also have to be careful that we aren't getting the cart ahead of the horse. In my brief research, I did not encounter anything suggesting that the Grange stands for membership growth. I'm not, certainly, saying membership growth is not important. But it's a cart that should naturally follow the horse of purpose. There are a few lines in the Declaration of Purposes that do include a subtle reference to membership growth.

"We propose meeting together, talking together, working together, and in general, acting together for our mutual protection and advancement. We shall constantly strive to secure harmony, good will, and brotherhood, and to make our Order perpetual. We shall earnestly endeavor to suppress personal, local, sectional, and national prejudices, all unhealthy rivalry and all selfish ambition. Faithful adherence to these principles will insure our mental, moral, social and material advancement."

If we do those things outlined (meeting together, working together...), we "make our Order perpetual" by attracting like-minded and like-purposed folks.

If we did have a clearly defined purpose—one that can have different emphasis locally; that's one of the beauties of a grassroots organization—and we were working within those principles... could we see that last sentence in the declaration of purposes being rewritten to read, "Faithful adherence to these principles will insure our mental, moral, social and material advancement as well as membership growth."

Groucho Marx is often credited with saying he wouldn't join an organization that would have him as a member. It's a funny thought but it makes the point that one factor in people's choices around affiliation and joining is about shared values. The early days of the Grange were quite heady and, most would agree, the explosive growth of the Grange was phenomenal. Certainly part of it was due to the passion of the founders and early leaders. But ultimately, people joined because of common purpose and values. And what Grangers did in practice reflected those values. They looked at what the Grange was trying to do and said, "Hey, I want to be part of that because I believe in it!"

"If you want to build a ship, don't drum up people to collect wood and don't assign them tasks and work, but rather teach them to long for the endless immensity of the sea."

Antoine de Saint-Exupery

Ritual Creates Consistency, Builds Trust

Merriam-Webster provides a simple definition of "ritual" as a formal ceremony or series of acts that are always performed in the same way. Ritual creates consistency and people value consistency. Consistency diminishes uncertainty and leads to trust. Trust in turn leads to influence.

Even if we haven't committed Grange Ritual to memory, all but the newest members know what *"The hour of labor has arrived and the work of another day demands our attention..."* means and at least in general, what will happen next. In ceremonies soon taking place around the state, *"Since God placed man on earth, agriculture has existed..."* will signal the beginning of the Officer Installation Ceremonies.

I suspect one of the reasons our founders developed an extensive Ritual was to create consistency. During the rapid explosion of the Grange, it certainly became important to achieve some level of consistency. They were so successful that to this day, many people's impression of the Grange reflects its beginnings. That is not a bad thing, certainly. Of course, there is the obvious downside that consistency means we stop paying attention and things become automatic.

There once was a long-term member who had served as chaplain for many years. When she spoke, it was a rapid-fire monotone that, quite frankly, my brain could not keep up with. Conversely, I will always remember certain portions of the degrees I was taught because they were given by another long-term member who seemed to genuinely enjoy sharing the lessons. (Let's not forget that the degrees are lessons and we are teaching!) To this day, I can see and hear him in a large part because he was a teacher and not just a reciter. In the truest form of the word, what we call "the Ritual" is about consistency and communication. Remembering the words is one thing; understanding the words is something else. What we say should be a reflection of what we do.

During Officer Installations, the master is invited to "open with an original address" but "should close with the following…" That's when we hear those familiar words *"Since God placed man on earth…"* Then, after reminding us of the importance of agriculture, the installing master shares some thoughts that I've often wished were part of every meeting. *"The Order of the Patrons of Husbandry is the only association whose teachings accompany its members in their daily pursuits."* If you have the good fortune to attend or participate in an Officer Installation Ceremony, let those words be a trigger and pay attention! The value of the Grange is not limited to meetings, the Ritual, and being at the Grange Hall. The value of the Grange can be found in our "daily pursuits."

There are many reasons the Grange was so successful in its early history—one is found in the fact that the "lessons of the Grange" were truly a way of life and it was a way of life that had appeal and value. Being a Granger was relevant not only at the hall but also in the field and community.

During a recent media interview, I was asked about the relevance of the Grange today given some of the changes in farming and agriculture. The interviewer seemed to be suggesting that those changes would, in fact, be a significant opportunity for the Grange. Several Community/Subordinate Granges in Maine are demonstrating that truth because their very existence and program are lightening and elevating the labor of their farmer members. Other Community/Subordinate Granges have recognized that our existence and program is not at all limited to farmers.

I often describe the Grange as "steeped in tradition, but

relevant for today" in a large part because the teachings of the Grange are no less needed now than 150 years ago. *"Honesty is inculcated, education nurtured, temperance supported, brotherly love cultivated, and charity made an essential characteristic."* Just looking at that one sentence—do individuals and society, in general, have a need for those teachings? Are the values of the Grange any less important and relevant today?

If you remain unconvinced, fast forward to the master's challenge at the close of Installation. *"And now, Patrons, carry with you a feeling of compassion for those who strive to make the world a better place. Let us work hand in hand for the good of our neighbors. Let us remember that those with trials and tribulations need our help most of all."*

Creating Balance, Remembering Values

In this month's Communication Column (you may want to read it first) I challenged readers to consider the question, "What if we rethink Grange?" That is a question that, unfortunately, may frighten traditionalists. But "rethinking" doesn't mean "abandoning."

There's a lot of polarity in the world today with lots of blacks and whites and very few shades of gray. There are also just too many "zero-sum games." Personally, I like the word "balance."

In working with the media, I find most often reporters' interest lies in the status of the Grange as an organization that is historical and perhaps irrelevant—one reason for decreasing membership and abandoned Grange Halls. This is one reason I keep asking Grangers to send news of exciting events and programs, especially the sort that create growth. The media reports, we create the stories.

Most of the stories that need to be publicized aren't made inside the Grange Hall with doors closed. The real stories are happening (or should be) in our communities. And, believe it or not, the real stories are based on some pretty "old" Grange stuff that's very relevant for today.

Several years ago, Walter Whitcomb, Maine Agriculture Commissioner, made a statement during a presentation at a Maine State Grange Conference that set me to thinking. This is not a direct quote, but what I remember him saying is "The values of the Grange have never been more important or necessary than they are today."

The purpose of a handshake is to convey trust, respect, balance, and equality. If it is done to form an agreement, the agreement is not official until the hands are parted. ("Let's shake on that.") We now have fist bumps and pinky promises—the act may change but the meaning does not. As Grangers, we need to remember that beneath the Ritual and traditions lie values and, if there's a question about our relevance in the world today the answer probably lies in those values.

We can change the way we express those values without abandoning them. In order to remain relevant, we may need to rethink how we express our values and how we "fit" in the world today. Without values and purpose, we lose relevancy. Halls are abandoned when they are no longer needed.

The master reminds us of our values when closing a Grange meeting. *"Brothers and Sisters, as we are again to separate and mingle with the world, let us not forget the principles of our Order. Let us add dignity to labor, and in our dealings with our fellow men, be honest, be just, and fear not. We must avoid intemperance in eating, drinking, and language, also in work and recreation, and whatever we do, strive to do well. Let us be quiet, peaceful citizens, feeding the hungry, helping the fatherless and the widows, and keeping ourselves unspotted from the world."*

"A Patron places faith in God, nurtures hope, dispenses charity and is noted for fidelity."

I dare you to try and tell me that's not relevant and needed.

Which Way Does the Welcome Mat Go?

We took an extra vacation this year! Don't worry, I'm not going to write about that. But in the course of that second trip, we reconnected with an old friend at a dulcimer concert in New York. The concert was held in a perhaps unusual venue—a large church complex.

While waiting for the concert there were plenty of opportunities to explore. Given my interest in communications, I found myself enjoying the many different messages posted and on tables with clipboards. This was clearly an active place with a number of systems in place to both manage the complex and the many programs offered.

One of the messages I found particularly interesting was "What if we rethink Church?" The questions were too many to list here but let me give you a taste. I've taken the liberty of changing "church" to "Grange."

- What if we rethink Grange—not in terms of what it is, but what it could be?

- What if all our Granges were active vibrant places where people wanted to be?

- What if Grange wasn't just a place to go, but something we do?

- What if we could offer the world a new vision that inspires faith, hope, charity, and fidelity? (For those who may miss the subtlety, this question is based on the Grange Salutation.)

Those seem like big challenges—at least at first. But if we pay attention to our heritage we know that small seeds can yield large crops.

And it's not a zero-sum game. Mary French, Director of the Dictionary Project wrote an interesting article in this summer's Dictionary Project Newsletter, "iPads vs Books." She makes a very convincing case for not abandoning the traditional paper and pencil and printed text. For us "older folk," it's comforting to hear the value of the tools we grew up with is still very real. But that doesn't mean we have to abandon technology either. Mary's article points out the importance of critical thinking. "What if" questions are part of that process.

During our road trip, we drove by a nameless library in a small town in Vermont. The front lawn included some nice shade trees with Adirondack-style chairs that invited one to sit and read. A restaurant we visited was decorated with artwork done by local school students. They weren't just taped to the wall, they were matted and framed giving the restaurant an "art gallery" feel. These are simple examples of rethinking. A library is more than a place to store books; a restaurant is more than a place to eat.

Returning to the church, I was particularly struck by an invitation to look at organization from the outside in, from the inside out, and upside down in order to develop "…a new understanding that opening our doors isn't just about letting people in, but about us going out and making personal connections in the world around us."

If you visit Janice and me at our home and are observant, you'll perhaps think our welcome mat is backward. Unless somebody has "fixed" it, I keep it placed so it says, "Welcome" as one is leaving. It's a perhaps silly and subtle way of communicating that the world is a pretty cool place to be with lots to offer.

What Are We Guarding and Why?

There is a story that tells how the Russian czar in 1903 noticed a sentry posted for no apparent reason in the midst of the Kremlin grounds. When he inquired of the captain of the guard, the czar was informed that in 1776 Catherine the Great found the first flower of spring blooming in that spot.

She commanded that a sentry would be posted to make certain no one trampled the flower.

Apparently, the order simply stood and so did a sentry—for the next 127 years.

It's a story that might be true. And some will chuckle at the irony of the thought that the spot was guarded mindlessly for over a century. The need for the sentry had obviously dissipated with the change of seasons. Why bother to guard a patch of bare ground?

I suspect few would argue that posting that sentry was not an efficient use of military resources. But as a self-appointed devil's advocate, I have to wonder. Now that we know why the sentry is there, isn't it great to be reminded that Catherine the Great noticed that flower and deemed it worthy of protection?

The story just might demonstrate the importance of not forgetting the meaning of the Ritual—or for that matter, habit. During that 127 years, an untold number of sentries did their duty. They didn't question why. So perhaps another lesson from the story is the importance of duty.

"Worthy Steward, are the gates properly guarded?

"They are, Worthy Master."

Why!?

During our recent Officer Installation, we had several children present. One eleven-year-old girl seemed interested in what was happening so I offered her a manual to "follow along" and several quick explanations. (I was not too surprised to receive an email from her later thanking me. I can well imagine how boring it could have been for her without some understanding of what was happening.) We didn't specifically discuss the Gatekeeper's duty. But during Installation, we learned,

"…I caution you to be vigilant and watchful. Your position between the Outer and Inner Gates is a responsible one. Neglect on your part might permit an enemy to enter, rob the orchard and vineyard, or sow the ground with tares. Being chosen by your fellow Patrons is evidence that they hold you in high esteem. Deserve it, by sleepless watchfulness at your post, by scrutinizing all who enter or pass out, by seeing that the garments of the Laborers are suitable, and that none enter the field except authorized persons, clad in proper attire."

(And, while you're at it, make sure nobody steps on those flowers.)

I occasionally hear of Granges where the Gatekeeper's role is being redefined as that of a greeter. No doubt this will become controversial in some circles—some will be certain that's "not what the founders had it mind." Personally, I think it's an interesting and much-needed shift—although in truest form every member should be a greeter, making guests feel comfortable. The question we might ask ourselves during the discussion is whether or not being a greeter is in conflict with being a Gatekeeper.

Perhaps having the conversation is the point. Should we—either as a lecturer's program or an item of business—be discussing our expectations of each of the officer roles in our Grange? We're nearing the end of the installation season—what a great time and place to start!

At your next meeting, pick an office, review the
Installation charge, and talk about how that office/officer
contributes to your Grange. Let's be vigilant but know
and remember what it is we're guarding.

Celebrating Traditions

Earlier this morning I was at school, conducting a kick-off assembly for the Valley Grange Bookworm Program. (For those unfamiliar, different Grangers visit the school twice a week to listen to second and third graders read.) We gathered together all the second and third graders to talk about the program. After a brief introduction of the program, I always ask the kids if they have any questions.

One young fellow raised his hand and asked, "How long have you been doing this?" Ironically, since I knew a reporter was going to attend, I'd looked that up—it's a favorite media question. The kids were quite impressed when I answered, "Ten years." I suppose ten years is a long time when you consider that meant we started the year most of those third graders were born!

He set me to thinking, though. Grange bookworms have become an important way of life at our school. The third graders visit the Valley Grange Hall every fall for a "Dictionary Day" that includes learning more about the Grange. Some of the kids that we've given dictionaries to and heard read are now graduating from high school. We have a number of traditions and many of our programs are seen as "rites of passage" at the school.

I sat with the kids we selected to be interviewed by the newspaper. One third grade girl provided me with an important reminder about tradition. When the reporter asked her what she liked best about the Bookworm Program she replied, "Well I like reading but I also like spending time with the Grangers." She then looked at me and asked, "Do you remember I read a joke book to you last year? I know you like them!" I didn't admit that I had no specific memory of it—those few minutes we had spent together were too important to her to dismiss them.

Tradition is defined in many different ways. One I

particularly like is given in Merriam-Webster Dictionary as "a way of thinking, behaving, or doing something that has been used by the people in a particular group, family, society, etc., for a long time."

The reporter and I chatted for a while after the kids left. He's been covering Valley Grange events for a long time and he admitted that sometimes it's hard to find a new headline or a new way of presenting the story of Bookworming or Dictionary Day. "But," he added, "it's always fun to hear the excitement from the kids—it's so new and important to them."

I found myself thinking, "Maybe we should let the kids write the story." But I also found myself realizing how important it is that we don't get caught in the trap of just going through the motions no matter how many times we've done something. Traditions have value but carry with them responsibility and opportunity. I truly can't guess how many kids I've taken from a classroom and listened to read over the last decade. But I do know that they keep track of when it's their turn and many remember the experience for a long time after.

I also don't know how many times I've been part of the opening or closing ritual in various offices. I'm not sure how many times I've been part of a degree day. But I do know that when we follow tradition and the Ritual it's easy to miss or forget the magic.

One of the harder questions I entertained from the kids was "Do we have to do this if we don't want to?" My answer was "No…" but as I was walking away from the questioner I stopped, turned around, and put on the saddest face I could and added, "But I will be really disappointed if you don't." Some might say I was being manipulative, but I really meant it. This is a tradition that we don't do just because it's a tradition. We do it because it's fun and it's meaningful and it makes a difference. It works because the reader and the person being read to both benefit. If we don't do it, we are cheating each other in the truest sense. And if we do it just for the sake of getting it done, that's not much better than not doing it at all.

Grange Ritual and practice should be no different. The Grange Way of Life is, I think, about celebration. We celebrate nature and agriculture, but also what they represent and the lessons we can learn from them.

Just as we challenge our bookworms to read, I challenge Grangers to engage in tradition and the Ritual in a new way. No matter how many times you've said or done it, next time make a special effort to make it fun and meaningful. Celebrate the Ritual! It will make a difference—to you and those around you.

A Quick Tip! Changing How We Talk

Maybe we should change the way we talk?

I've written before about how we refer to the Ritual and degree work–and I know how difficult it is to change habits. But what would happen if we tried to change the way we refer to both? We currently have a number of different expressions like "We are <u>doing</u> the Ritual" and "Have you <u>taken</u> the degrees?"

Should we, could we instead say things like "We are celebrating the Ritual!" and "Have you celebrated the degrees?"

Linguists tell us that language often reflects the way we think, but it's also true that the way we talk affects the way we think. One reason I've never particularly liked the question "Have you taken (or received) the degrees?" is that it's passive and suggests the degrees are something that happens to someone. I believe the degrees are a celebration of agriculture and what it teaches us!

I'm not going to change the title of my column–it's long enough already. But we really should be "Exploring and celebrating the Grange Way ofLlife." It's awesome!

P.S. I didn't change the title of my column but I did change the title of this book!

Emblems for Classroom Management

For several years I've used our staves as part of our Valley Grange Dictionary Day visits—whether the kids visit us at the Grange Hall or we visit their classrooms. They have always seemed to enjoy learning about these "farmer's tools" and often will mention them when they write thank you notes. Occasionally a student will accurately draw each of the four. When that happens, I confess to wondering if we Grangers can remember all four? I hope so because I also explain to these third graders why we use them in our meetings. Historically that explanation has been a general one. This year I decided to be a bit more specific and I turned to the officer Installation Ceremony for help.

"Your emblem is the Spud, an ancient implement used by Stewards in passing through the fields to eradicate weeds that may have escaped the notice of the laborers... Let it remind you of your duty as a faithful steward to remove all causes of dissension or strife, in the Grange and in order." When I've explained to the kids that all Grangers see the spud as a reminder to keep the Grange free of weeds, they offer what some of the things are they as classmates, might want to eliminate for their classroom. Their answers often include "bullying" and "bad words."

"Your emblem is the Pruning Hook. The spear, beaten into a pruning hook is emblematic of peace. May it always remind you of your duty to preserve peace in our order..." There's a natural progression here. My dictionary day helpers know the staves must be in the "right" order before I began—not just because of tradition, but because it makes sense. When we eliminate bad things (dissension and strife or bullying and bad words) we begin building peace.

"I present you, the Lady Assistant Steward of your

 children takes some editorial license, in part because we have fun with this "tool." I'll select a volunteer to be a sheep and demonstrate how the shepherd uses the crook "like a leash" to guide the sheep. The application is, therefore, that seeing the crook reminds us that we each can be a leader, guiding others in our efforts to remove "weeds" and "build peace."

The kids love the owl; he's almost everybody's favorite stave. When I remove him from the stand, someone always shouts, "He's cute!" (The one I use is wooden and quite realistic in appearance.) Upon receiving it, the Gatekeeper is told *"I caution you to be vigilant and watchful"* with a comparatively lengthy explanation of the dangers to be kept from our Order. Usually, the kids can come up with why a farmer might like an owl to "scare away birds and mice." In the Grange, the owl reminds us to see what's around us, both to enjoy beauty but also to protect by removing dissension…

I confess the first time I tried this it was unrehearsed and probably didn't hang together as well as it could and now does. As a teacher, for the first time I saw these four staves as potential classroom management tools—even joking with one class that it's too bad they don't have a set like we do—or maybe a photo poster of them. (I can picture a kid going to a corner of the room, grabbing a spud, marching over to another kid and saying, "You used an inappropriate word! That's not allowed!" I also confess that I now see the staves a bit different myself. These staves represent tools that we must use constantly to preserve our Order, an Order that strives to remove dissension and strife, build peace and caring, and develop vigilance and watchfulness.

"The Order of the Patrons of Husbandry is the only association whose teachings accompany its members in

While the literal staves may remain in the holders between meetings, what they represent should accompany us in our daily pursuits. I would encourage (uh oh, sounds like we're going to get some homework!) each member to find or borrow a Grange Manual and read/study the installing officer's opening address. That address describes some of the reasons we need those staves—not just for four people to hold and carry during the Ritual but as a way of life.

Don't Use That Fork!

"Nothing more rapidly inclines a person to go into a monastery than reading a book on etiquette. There are so many trivial ways in which it is possible to commit some social sin."

Quentin Crisp

Isn't that an interesting thought? Some years ago, I was contacted by a major pharmaceutical company who requested "etiquette" training for their sales force. They were concerned about this very point and wanted to be certain salespeople knew which fork to use at formal dinners for fear of committing a social sin that would alienate prospective customers (mostly doctors).

The story of that program is interesting. A short version brings us to the point that choosing the fork wasn't the real issue. There were some far more basic "etiquette" issues (like not listening to and respecting those potential customers) that needed to be addressed.

Most people will forgive us for using the wrong utensil at a dinner. (The principles of etiquette are based on the assumption that behaving properly communicates respect.) It falls under the heading of a trivial way of committing some social sin. Most would agree, there's a difference between failing to hold a door open because we didn't notice someone behind us versus slamming the door in his or her face.

In previous columns, I have written about the importance of celebrating our traditions and Ritual along with the importance of keeping them in perspective and balance. The Ritual is also about communication and, I think, very analogous to etiquette because both our words and actions form our language.

I think the author's point is similar to the one I have tried to make. While I'm not an expert on etiquette, I know that he's right. If you thoroughly read a book on etiquette you might be frightened at the number of often trivial ways one can commit a social sin.

How different is that with our own Grange "etiquette?" Ours is complicated by the fact that much of it is not "written down" or readily available from a dependable source. I once sat in a meeting that included a twenty-minute debate among self-appointed experts on which foot to lead with during some floorwork. I have attended meetings and degree work when memorized parts were rattled off so fast and with so little feeling they were unintelligible. We might well consider what actions like this communicate.

Obsessive attention to detail in the Ritual will sometimes send people running from our Granges. Would you want to sit next to someone at a formal dinner who kept pointing out your errors in selection of utensils and how to place them to signal the server your intentions? Just this week I heard yet another story of the Grange equivalent of that happening. A member arrived at a meeting late and either didn't know or couldn't remember the "correct" procedure for "working in" to a meeting. The way he was treated sent him, almost literally, running from the Grange. No, he didn't enter a monastery, but in spite of the fact his family was deeply involved in Grange, he has never attended another meeting since.

So perhaps instead of focusing on the "trivial ways" we have, we might look at the values of the Grange. At the beginning of the Third Degree, the steward explains to the candidates (my emphasis), *"…should possess your minds that you may <u>enjoy your advancement</u> and feel as well as hear the attendant lessons. <u>We must reap for the mind as well as for the body</u>, and from the abundance of our harvest, <u>in good deeds and kind words dispense charity.</u>"*

Counting Seeds Is Easy

Most Grangers I talk with admit that the first time they celebrated the four degrees, the event was a bit of a blur and the instruction they received wasn't fully appreciated. It is certainly interesting to ask Grangers to recite one or two things they distinctly remember from that experience.

One of my distinct memories happened during the Second Degree when the master showed us a few kernels of corn in his hand. I remember watching his fingers move as he explained, *"We are now to teach you how to plant the seed. Behold these inanimate kernels of corn! But the germ has life – the future plant is there. We loosen the soil – we bury the seed; and in so doing impress upon our minds the truth of the immortality of the soul. There is no object in which, to appearance, life and death border so closely together as in the grains of seed buried in the earth; but when life seems extinct a fuller and richer existence begins anew."*

Those words and thoughts can be a great comfort to us in times of sorrow. But the lesson of the seeds has nearly endless application. I have occasionally used an apple to make a similar point. (This might be a short lecturer's program!) I will hold up an apple and ask, "How many seeds are in this apple?" Most people will not know, so we may actually cut it open and count them. One of those seeds can then be selected and another question poised. "How many apples are in this seed?"

"Anyone can count the number of seeds in an apple… but only God can count the number of apples in a seed."

-Robert Schuller

The lesson of the apple seed is the lesson of the kernel of corn—each contains unlimited potential. *"From this*

Later, in the same degree, the Master instructs, "*May the lessons you have received find genial soil in your minds. Cultivate with hope the seed thus planted, that it may yield an hundred fold.*"

The lessons of the Grange are the lessons of agriculture. Nature can teach us much if we listen and much of our Grange tradition and instruction encourages us to listen and learn those lessons.

Ceres explains, *"As we look around and see the beautiful transformation of seeds into attractive plants or majestic trees, we have but another lesson taught us of the wondrous works of God. Changes and transformations are constantly passing before us — the dying grain into the living stalk, the tiny seeds into majestic trees, the bud to blossom, the blossom to fruit. All these preach eloquently of the wonder-working God; and if the beauties of this world, when rightly viewed, offer so much of the magnificence of the Creator to charm us here, what must be the sublime grandeur of that Paradise above, not made with hands, eternal in the heavens?"*

I recall a news anchor's comment following a story about Valley Grange's Words for Thirds Program. He'd observed how excited the kids were about dictionaries and reading and closed his segment by saying, simply, "There is hope." All of the lessons of the Grange seem to bring us inescapably to that one word–hope.

We are challenged to consider the words we say, the gifts we give, the simple actions we take as seeds. They are the germs of life. The future lies in them, even when we can't see it. We are planting hope.

Pressing Forward

"We are constantly passing blindly along the pathway of life, events occurring that we do not understand, and often encountering difficulties and obstructions in our way; but we should press forward, having Faith that God will ultimately bring us into broad and pleasant fields of paradise."

The master's observation to First Degree candidates is certainly of interest to an organization steeped in history and tradition. For one hundred fifty years, Patrons of Husbandry have survived passing along the pathway of life, perhaps not totally blindly, but certainly encountering events we did not often understand. There can be little doubt that we have encountered difficulties and obstructions along our way and will continue to do so. For our organization, the key phrase is "we should press forward."

Pressing forward does not equal abandoning the past. But it does mean that we must face those difficulties and obstructions while being good stewards without clinging unreasonably to the past and tradition but also without abandoning the basic beliefs and practices that have and will continue to serve us well. We do that as individuals, should we do any less as an organization?

As I study these words, it occurs to me that this might be meant to describe a process—one that is cyclical and repeats itself—just as do the seasons of the year. There are, in fact, "broad and pleasant fields of paradise" along the pathway that includes "difficulties and obstructions."

Later, in the same degree, the master uses the analogy of grass to challenge the candidates to consider "man's transitory state upon earth and also of a brighter and more glorious truth."

This lesson of this degree gives us much to consider. While introducing this lesson, the master holds a bundle of dried grasses as a visual aid. *"This bouquet as you perceive, is composed wholly of different varieties of grasses, possessing little beauty and less of interest to the careless observer, but full on instruction to the receiving mind."*

As we open our minds to consider the lesson, we must immediately recognize the renewal quality of grass. As the snow melts, here in Maine, we see brown. But soon it will awaken. I liken this to getting past the difficulties and obstructions we face and arriving into broad and pleasant fields.

But for some reason, the words "does not each tiny spear, as it shoots from the ground…" looked different to me when I saw them this time, perhaps because I was for the first time seeing this as it applies not only to us as individuals, but also as an organization. I suddenly saw each member as a "tiny spear" of grass. I also saw those spears shooting from the ground in a way of renewal that would create a broad and pleasant field of paradise.

That brings us to the word "Faith." We must believe in ourselves and our Order. We will keep celebrating birthdays if we believe we can and follow the lessons our founders gave us.

Hope Versus Belief

"The question has been asked, 'How long will the Grange live?' I believe it will live as long as it continues to serve the welfare of agriculture and the nation. Whenever it becomes ingrown and selfish, and the members look on it only as a means of bringing them pleasure, entertainment, or profit, it will fade away."

Those words for today were actually written and spoken in the 1940's by then National Master Albert S. Goss.[1]

One of the pointed questions asked during our Piscataquis Pomona town hall meeting with National Master Betsy Huber was, "Given we are a diverse, grassroots organization, what really unites us?" The question may be as important as the answer because the question drives us back to our roots and fundamental principles and policies.

Ironically, just a few days later, a member of the media asked me, "What is your hope for the Grange?" It was one of the few times I didn't have a prepared soundbite for a reply. After fumbling a bit, I answered, "that it continues to be a vibrant and energetic organization that contributes to our communities." Feeling that I hadn't exactly given a great answer, it was that question which later made me pull down some of my Grange books and do some reading and thinking.

Master Goss's hope can be found in the second paragraph. "But to those who find pleasure in doing something for the common good, the Grange provides an instrument both effective and satisfying. Through it, we can jointly find our entertainment and our pleasure in service, while at the same time we can advance the interests of our neighbors and ourselves in the fields of health, education, business and in almost limitless ways. Through the Grange we have an opportunity to give, and the more we give the more we gain."

If the reporter who interviewed me had the ability to interview Master Goss, I suspect he would have used a redirect in his reply to the reporter's question, "What is your hope for the Grange?" I think that the Master might have replied that he had a belief, not a hope. There's an important difference between those two words. Master Goss believed, "…it will still be the motivating center from which unlimited community welfare enterprises originate; and it will continue to build and strengthen the farm home as its ultimate purpose."

One of the many strengths of our Order is an almost uncanny ability to look to the past as we move to the future. When we talk about our Granges, we too often get focused on today's challenges like how hard it is to get members or the need to "close" for the winter to avoid a heating bill. Perhaps it is time to explore our traditions and our history of success. In the same book, I found Master Goss's prophecy, I stumbled on to this statement: "The Grange has lived and will live because it is founded on the home, the family, and the farm."

Is that any less true today, some seventy-five years later? Will we continue to live because we are founded on the home, the family, and the farm? One of the reasons I decided to write this "Exploring Traditions…" column every month is my belief that much of our history, heritage, tradition, and practice has application for today—if we are willing and able to understand and apply it.

There's a song that will be familiar to many… "He's an old hippie and he don't know what to do… should he hang on to the old or grab on to the new?" Perhaps we could change one word and make it our opening song at an occasional meeting. "He's an old Granger and he don't know what to do… should he hang on to the old or grab on to new?"

The problem is the question is an absolute, implying

there's a required a choice between the old and the new. I don't know about hippies, but Grangers do not need to make an either-or choice. We need to hang on to the old to the extent it makes sense and to the degree it got us where we are. But we also need to grab on to the new if we are going to "be the motivating center from which unlimited community welfare enterprises originate."

Do you share Master Goss's belief? Can you see a sign over the door to your Grange Hall that reads, "Welcome to the motivating center from which unlimited community welfare enterprises originate!" That's better than "closed for the winter."

---

[1] Gardner, C. M. (1949). *The Grange — Friend of the Farmer.* Washington DC: National Grange of the Patrons of Husbandry.

It's Just Something I Do

"The Order of Patrons of Husbandry is the only association whose teachings accompany its members in their daily pursuits. They form part of the farmer's life. They do not call him from his work to put his mind upon any other subject, but furnish recreation in his daily duties, and by cheerful instruction, lighten and elevate his labor."

We will be hearing those words again soon during the Installation of Officers. What a wonderful reminder of an important aspect of our Order—it is meant to be part of our daily lives—not something reserved for meetings at the Grange Hall.

I suspect one of the reasons our founders included this observation in the Installation Ceremony was to remind leaders of the importance of not interfering with members' daily labor but to furnish recreation and by cheerful instruction, lighten and elevate his daily labor.

While we tend to think of labor as "work," at least one dictionary defines it as "productive activity." I think it's interesting how our view of that has changed over the years. I'm currently reading a book about a farmer who labored in the mid-late 1800's. I'm impressed with all the things he did, but never get the sense he considered himself busy. He worked with the seasons, doing the things that needed doing. The author, his grandson, explains his grandfather's explanation often was, "it's just something I do." His work was his life and his life was his work. I think farmers today would agree it's still not an "eight to five" job.

Small wonder the Grange is such a great organization for farmers. Being a Grange member is not about attending a meeting or two every month. Much like farming, being a Granger is an around-the-clock activity. Or at least it's meant to be! The master's entire opening comments emphasize that Grange is not supposed to interfere with our lives; it is truly meant to enhance and enrich our lives. And the task of those who lead the Order is to make sure that happens.

One of the reasons our Order is about to celebrate 150 years of existence is, I believe, the fact that it remains relevant and does enhance and enrich members' lives. When the Bangor Daily News Reporter asked me what my hope was for the Grange of the future, I replied: "that every Grange finds a way to be a viable, energetic resource for their community, however that community is defined." When we look at those Granges experiencing membership growth they have done that, but their growth and success is not solely about the programs they are doing.

In that same interview, I suggested that growing Granges always have two common qualities: good leadership and lots of passion. In growing Granges, members aren't putting their lives on hold to "go to Grange" because Grange is part of their life. Their membership does furnish recreation, but it also means that by cheerful instruction (which includes networking) they are finding their labor (lives) lightened and elevated.

Simple things are not always easy. The installing master also observes, *"Thus our Order binds us together in fraternity…"* I think it's important to note that he or she does not say, "Our fraternity binds us together in our Order…" What really binds us together is a shared vision and purpose. In the absence of that, there is no reason to trudge to the Grange Hall for a meeting—particularly on a cold or rainy night.

While it may be tempting to think life was simpler 150 years ago, let's remember that those early Grangers didn't hop in a car and turn the key while checking in with others in the family on a smartphone. Consider the effort it must have taken—chores had to be completed, the horse and wagon readied… but that effort was done without complaint. Going to Grange was as much a part of their lives as doing those chores. They came from far and wide because it mattered.

A Loving Touch, a Way of Life

It recently became my sad privilege (notice I did not say "duty") to serve once again as the chaplain in a Grange Burial Service. Bill Bemis, Master of Garland Grange and Piscataquis Pomona, and I actually make a pretty good team. We've had far more practice than we'd like and rehearsals are no longer necessary. Bill always remembers the ribbons and flowers and other than a few quick exchanges before we start, things seem to proceed smoothly At this most recent, the funeral director thanked us profusely for so serving. Since several of our services have been with him, he's part of the team as well.

Many of the traditions surrounding death and burial are shifting and in some cases being forgotten. We can debate whether or not this is a good thing, but my experience has been that most people find many of the "old" practices comforting and respectful.

The Grange Burial Service can, of course, be found in the Subordinate Grange Manual. There is no need for memorization—even ministers and other professionals who perform services frequently tend to use their manuals—if only for support during what is surely a difficult time when it can be easy to lose one's place and thoughts. We are driven by a desire to support the family and friends. That, above all, determines what is correct.

There are, by the way, some significant differences between the service found in older manuals when compared to the "new" manual issued in 2013. In all honestly, I greatly prefer the older version for several reasons.

The 2013 version is significantly shorter than the previous. While burials should be relatively brief, the brevity of the 2013 version is achieved by omitting much. I suspect the 2013 version would, even at a slow pace, only last several minutes! More importantly, the 2013 version seems to omit or shorten many of the "lessons" offered in the older version—lessons that offer important comfort and reflection.

Another difference is that the 2013 version omits the hymns and singing—and that is supported by generally accepted practice. I cannot remember the last time I was at a burial service of any type where attendees were asked to sing. When conducting the Grange service, I will often recite the words to the suggested songs as poetry.

The most important considerations are the family's preferences and what the acting chaplain and master are comfortable with. Both manuals make it clear the service is optional. Given the fluidity in today's practices, there is some room for "customizing." While I do not think it is appropriate to conduct long eulogies as part of a burial service, I will offer a few brief comments or a pleasant memory of the deceased to ensure that the service is delivered in a way that is truly about him or her.

To that point, many people (Grangers included) are not aware or will forget during times of trouble that there is such a thing as a Grange Burial Service. The Subordinate Grange Manual also includes a "Grange Service for Private Home or Funeral Home." There is certainly no requirement that these be conducted for a deceased Granger, those who remain would perhaps like to know that the Grange can support and help. There is a requirement for draping the charter, also included in the Subordinate Grange Manual. It is entirely appropriate to remind our brothers and sisters of these services and other support the Grange may provide such as hosting family and friends after a service.

This column is certainly not mean to be morbid—it is offered as a reminder that our traditions demonstrate how there is a Grange Way of Life (and in this case, death). While traditions change and society develops, the Grange remains relevant and viable.

I would challenge chaplains to fully explore your duties and opportunities. If you are re-elected or newly elected this month, listen carefully to the charge you are given during Installation *"…to be faithful to your calling… may the spiritual seed you shall sow fall on good soil, and bring forth an hundredfold. Cast thy bread upon the waters, and thou shalt gather it after many days…"*

In the alternate Installation Ceremony, chaplains are instructed more specifically, *"When it becomes necessary, you will conduct a memorial service to honor members who have gone on before us. Your loving touch will add to the ceremony…"*

The chaplain should be assisted by every member as we labor together to support each other in times of sadness and in times of joy. We should bring a "loving touch" to all our work together. When we conduct the "altar circle" during the induction of new members, the master promises, *"…we pledge to you our friendship… a pure friendship, enduring through life, to shield you from harm…"* That's a great way of life.

Seeking a Fuller and Richer Experience

"…The springing seed teaches us to increase in goodness, and the growing trees to aspire after higher and broader knowledge." These are words spoken by the Chaplain during the celebration and instruction of the Second Degree.

Later in the degree, the Master explains, *"There is no object in which, to appearance, life and death border so closely together as in the grains of seed buried in the earth; but when life seems extinct a fuller and richer existence begins anew."* Near the close of this degree, the master reminds us that *"The salutation of this degree 'places faith in God and nurtures Hope."*

Grange Ritual and teachings take great advantage of the lessons of nature and those lessons are many. *"The tools used by us in this degree are the hoe and the pruning knife. The hoe, with which we cut up weeds and stir the soil, is emblematic of that cultivation of the mind which destroys error and keeps our thoughts quickened and ready to receive new facts as they appear, thus promoting the growth of knowledge and wisdom."*

"The pruning knife, used to remove useless and injurious growths from our trees, plants and vines, should remind you to prune idle thoughts and sinful suggestions… Bear in mind that moral and metal worth rank before worldly wealth or honors…"

I wish I could remember where I recently read the observation that "in order to become a butterfly, you have to be willing to give up being a caterpillar." The words are not exactly Grange teaching, but the thought surely is. *"When life seems extinct a fuller and richer existence begins anew."*

If you have some remaining seeds from planting your garden (the Second Degree uses corn) I'd encourage you to find one and hold it in your palm and hear the master's words, *"Behold these inanimate kernels of corn! But the germ has life – the future plant is there…"* In a workshop I've presented, I point out that all of the life potential and a complete set of instructions to create it are within that small seed. That's H-O-P-E and a powerful lesson nature teaches.

The lesson is certainly about individual potential, but I think it can apply to our Granges which, after all, are a collection of individuals. If each of us has that much promise and potential, does not our Grange? When we consider our heritage, our principles, and our teachings… do we not have within us the potential for a *"fuller and richer existence…"* are not all the instructions there that will allow us to grow into something wonderful? Is our Order placing faith in God and nurturing hope? Are we collectively increasing in goodness and aspiring after higher and broader knowledge?

I wonder what a caterpillar thinks—or for that matter, if it does. Does it know what its future is going to be? Nature clearly has programmed it to wrap itself up in a mummy-like state without questioning whether or not it's a good idea. The caterpillar doesn't have to decide to give up its existence and become a butterfly. That's a grand plan because if caterpillars were like people, the situation would be a lot different. Many caterpillars would be quite content to remain caterpillars. Some would fear becoming a butterfly and needing to fly. They would be quite content to crawl about munching leaves. But some would look forward to the adventure and the freedom that comes with flying. They would be willing to go through the metamorphosis required. Those who remain caterpillars would cling to their existence and perhaps even complain that there aren't enough caterpillars left because everyone is too busy being a butterfly.

The Grange way of life, like nature, is meant to be filled with hope, promise, and potential. We just have to decide to give up being caterpillars and commit to becoming a butterfly—to becoming something that is different and beautiful. The challenge we face is accepting that who and what we are may not be who and what we become. But let nature remind us that while the butterfly is found in the caterpillar, it is equally true that the caterpillar is found in the butterfly. Nature does not resist change, it depends on it, understanding that a seed is not meant to stay a seed and a caterpillar is not meant to remain a caterpillar. Life is about becoming and when we think things are dying what is really happening is. *"a fuller and richer existence begins anew."*

Why Aren't We Tapping Our Toes?

Seth Godin recently wrote[1] that it is not so much science and DNA that determines who or what we become, but culture does. He notes that our DNA is basically the same as a Cro-Magnon's and, "The reason you don't act the way they did is completely the result of culture, not genes." It's an interesting thought, yes? It becomes even more interesting when we consider the relationship of culture and tradition. It becomes powerful when we realize we may not be able to change our DNA, but we can change our culture.

Our recent vacation to Canada included a significant amount of drive time enabling us to consider what we were seeing and experiencing. One of our goals for the trip was to experience as much Celtic Music as was practical. We accomplished that by attending a number of Ceilidhs—the one Gaelic word we mastered during our stay. It's pronounced "Kay-lee" and we were truly amazed by what seemed an endless number of possible ones to attend. A Ceilidh is defined by Wikipedia as "a traditional Scottish or Irish social gathering. In its most basic form, it simply means a social visit. In contemporary usage, it usually involves playing Gaelic folk music and dancing, either at a house party or a larger concert at a social hall or other community gathering place." We found that the best Ceilidhs including some storytelling and jokes.

These Ceilidhs come in all sizes and shapes with enough diversity to keep one's interest for a long time. They are held in various venues including restaurants, pubs, barns, and even street corners. Nova Scotia is also dotted with Parish Halls that might be best described as "community centers." But "center" is certainly relative. We were

---

[1] **https://seths.blog/2017/08/sloppy-science/**

warned that one of the best Ceilidhs in the area is almost impossible to find. The best way for a non-local to go is to attend an earlier Ceilidh at a local restaurant, then follow the crowd when they leave and head towards Glencoe.

We couldn't help making some comparisons to Grange Halls in the United States—at least the Grange Halls of days past where "social gatherings" included suppers, music, and dancing. Their purposes actually are historically quite similar.

I came to the conclusion our Granges should consider having some events resembling Ceilidhs while attending one at a small restaurant called "The Red Shoe Pub." I feared it would be a tourist trap. The line outside the door reinforced my fears but in short order I found myself having fun, visiting with other people in line. We could hear the music. We could smell the food. The anticipation was almost over-powering. Inside, it got even better. It might be a stretch to suggest that we were "one big happy family" but we were a community immersed in a culture and tradition.

When the lead musician asked each table to tell where they were from it was apparent we were a global community with more folks coming from far than near. We were sitting at a table with a couple from Montreal, but at the table next to us were some "locals" with a toddler who could barely walk, but when the music played, he did his best to "step dance."

The words rang true. "we act the way we do as a result of culture." While I haven't had a DNA test, I'm reasonably certain there's not much Irish or Scottish blood in my heritage. But that night it felt like there was! Just about everyone's toes were tapping—there was much laughter and shouted conversation. (Two of the pub rules are "Don't ask for the wifi password," and "Drink lots of beer.") But it's not just the music and it's certainly not just the beer—several of the Ceilidhs we attended served only tea and biscuits. It's simply hard not to enjoy the Celtic Way of Life when you are sitting at a Ceilidh.

So there might be a question in all this for us. Remember: we can't change our DNA, but we can change our culture. What is the Grange Way of Life? Why aren't we dancing (literally and figuratively) more? Shouldn't we at least be tapping our toes? It should be hard not to enjoy the Grange Way of Life when you're sitting in a Grange Hall.

All Is Secure!

As part of my work with our school, I recently chaperoned a group of honor music students on a bit of a "field trip." They took part in a long day that culminated with a truly amazing concert. There were some twenty schools represented—middle school age kids. My job was basically to keep the kids safe and make sure they had a good time. For various reasons, I was in contact with our school principal several times throughout the day, most often by text message.

How does this relate to the Grange Way of Life? The experience demonstrated that as we adopt the "Grange Way" it can, in fact, become a way of life. We follow it and it follows us. I realized it after the concert was over and each student had, as instructed, "checked out" with me by bringing a parent to meet me before leaving. After the last one left, I texted the principal, "All is secure. Every student has checked out with a parent." At least I didn't call her "Worthy Master."

It's interesting that National Grange has adopted "The Grange Way" as a theme and I am anxious to see how that theme translates into practice, partly because of the challenges we face as a collection of individuals, trying to live the Grange Way. A strength of the Grange is also a weakness. As a grassroots organization, we take on many different forms and interests. Do we have an identity crisis?

What is the Grange Way? I confess I'm tempted to set up a survey on the website and ask that question. I suspect we'd get some interesting answers!

National Communications Director Amanda Brozana Rios revealed her new tattoo at the Maine State Grange Convention. On the inside of her forearm you 'll find the familiar, "In essentials, unity. In non-essentials, freedom, In all things, charity." I think that bit of ink represents a strong commitment to the Grange Way of Life and I congratulate Amanda for quite literally making it part of her.

While it makes sense to adopt new themes, and occasionally change our focus, for an organization such as ours, we do well when we consider what has worked for 150 years.

I think it's funny that I ended my school assignment with an automatic announcement, "All is secure." I think it would be great if we found ourselves reciting the Grange slogan more often. When we find ourselves disagreeing regarding a course of action during a Grange Meeting, someone needs to stand up and remind us, "In essentials, unity… in non-essentials, freedom… in all things charity." Is it necessary (essential) that we agree on everything? Can we allow individuality? How do we demonstrate charity (love) as we go about being Granges and Grangers?

You can bet you'll be hearing more from me on this topic… but for now, "All is secure."

We Get What We Deserve

(This month's offering may at first appear a bit "off track," but it is about tradition… it's actually a column I wrote for my "Brain Leaks" website [2]. I decided to adapt and share it here partly because I learned this lesson at a Grange Pomona Meeting and partly because I think when we look at the Grange and its Rituals and traditions, it's similarly true: We get the Grange we deserve.)

At our elementary school's Holiday Concert, one kindergartener was completely dressed in a Santa Suit! I couldn't resist looking totally shocked and saying to him, "Omigosh I didn't realize Santa was going to be here!"

He smiled at me, placed his hands on his little padded belly and said quite seriously, "Mr. Boomsma, what would you like for Christmas?" A few hours later I realized how important his question was.

Following the concert, I attended our Piscataquis Pomona Meeting where Pomona Lecturer Dave Pearson introduced us to a Christmas Song I'd never heard before. I'm not sure how I missed this song–it was written in 1974 by Greg Lake as a protest against the commercialization of Christmas. The song has an interesting history, but it has an even more interesting closing line:

"We get the Christmas we deserve…"

That's something to think about. We are, unfortunately, a culture of fault-finders and that makes us often feel victimized. We complain about how commercial Christmas has become… object to the costs and the

---

[2] **http:wboomsma.com/**

endless attempts at political correctness. We remember fondly the Christmases of yesteryear and whine, "It's not like it used to be."

Lake wrote the song in part because, as he described it, "Christmas was a time of family warmth and love. There was a feeling of forgiveness, acceptance. And I do believe in Father Christmas."

So maybe we need to focus on what we believe in and then ask ourselves "What am I contributing to the season and what do I want from it?" Once we've wrapped our heads (and hearts) around that we can create the activities that contribute to that meaning and focus on those. What **do** you want for Christmas? How are you going to get it?

Christmas isn't something that happens to us. We get the Christmas we deserve.

Is There Work for All?

Regular followers will remember that last month's column reflected on the truth, "We get the Christmas we deserve." As I paged through the manual for inspiration for this month's, it was perhaps fate that directed me to the Fourth Degree where the secretary addresses the candidates. After reminding them of the importance of punctuality, the secretary points out *"there is work for all,"* and adds *"those reap the most abundant harvest of Grange benefits [are those] who contribute most liberally of their own time and talent."*

We might well wonder if our secretary is suggesting "We get the Grange we deserve." The challenge is reminiscent of the analogy of sowing and reaping. If we sow our time and talent liberally in our Grange, we shall harvest abundantly. That could be a sobering thought for anyone who is questioning or unhappy with what he or she is "getting out" of membership. That unhappy member may be getting the Grange he or she deserves.

However, in fairness, we should also consider the accuracy of the statement, "There is work for all." Is there? There's got to be more going on than just meetings in order for there to be work for all.

Assuming there is work to do, it's commonly accepted that one good membership retention technique is to get and keep new members involved. I'd like to go one further.

There's an old joke about the pig and the hen walking down the road together. The topic of breakfast (bacon and eggs) comes up. The pig points out that all that's required of the hen is involvement. For the pig, commitment is required.

The founders of the Grange recognized the importance of purpose and demonstrated insight into how to build an effective organization. It's hard to get people involved in purposelessness. It's impossible to gain commitment without purpose. With clear purpose, it should become equally clear that there is work for everyone. If there is no purpose, then there is no work. It would be like asking people to show up to weed a garden where nothing has been planted!

Another insight of our founders was building a grassroots organization. While the umbrella is important, each Subordinate/Community Grange gets to create their own image--an opportunity that does encourage commitment. Personally, I believe the diversity in our Order is one of our biggest strengths. We can say with confidence, "There is work for all," because our organization is built to accommodate different passions.

We're not just for farmers. Just look at a committee list and consider the opportunities ranging from community service, healthy living, women's activities… to children/juniors… legislative matters… and we're not really limited to those. There are several Granges in Maine that have theatre companies. There can be engaging and rewarding work for all in any Grange.

Marrying Tradition to Today

I'm in the process of reading a very interesting book, _Josiah for President_. It raises the question, "Can a plain man of faith… become the leader of America?" I'm at the point where a former congressman has given up his campaign for president and by happenstance meets Josiah, an Old-order Amishman. Clearly, the question suggests that tradition and today are going to collide and our former congressman is going to consider Josiah running for president. (If I've raised your curiosity, the book is written by Martha Bolton and published Zondervan, Grand Rapids, MI in 2012.)

One of the reasons this book has been on my list for a while is my interest in the Amish. Another is the Grange's ongoing challenge of reconciling tradition and today. That challenge is not limited to the Grange, certainly. Our entire political system faces it, along with us and other organizations. (I am now encouraged to purchase Girl School cookies online.) Consider how many current political debates have their roots in today versus tradition. Should we abandon the electoral college? Does the thinking of our forefathers when they included the "right to bear arms" still apply in the different world we live in?

There's no doubt a keen value of the Grange over history has been its role in promoting the interests of agriculture, defending the welfare of rural people, and supporting good government. Many presidents have expressed support for the Grange throughout its history. Franklin D. Roosevelt was a Granger and explained, "For many years I have been a member of the Grange. I have felt at home in it because it embodies the fine flavor of rural living, which I myself have known and loved. Beyond this, it has been an instrument for expressing in useful activity the highest sentiments and deepest loyalties of Americans." (President Roosevelt received his Silver

Star certificate in 1939—he had been invested with the honor of the Seventh Degree in 1930.)

I think Roosevelt's explanation of his membership raises an interesting question for all members: "What is it about the Grange that makes us 'feel at home?" One of the reasons that might be an interesting and important question is that it requires us to learn more about the Grange and ourselves.

When my brother (who was unfamiliar with the Grange) visited several years ago, I dragged him along on a trip to the Grange Hall where I needed to perform some maintenance-related task. He and I share a love of antiques and old things, so I was pretty sure he'd appreciate the building and some of its furnishings—I left him to explore while I performed my task. When it was time to leave, I found him sitting in the foyer looking transfixed. He said, "Can't you just picture some old bearded farmers sitting here, gathered around the stove, talking?" I could. They looked very much "at home." The Grange was the place to meet with like-minded people--not just for the sake of meeting, but for the social opportunity to be with like-minded people in a supportive and sharing way.

Since his visit, the wood stove has been removed by order of the insurance company. But when we have a meeting or community program, people still gather on the porch in the summer or under the heating ducts in the winter. I have always been fascinated by how nearly everyone wants to help when we start cleaning up after a potluck supper. There's a warmth that doesn't come from the sun or the furnace. It might be the "fine flavor of rural living" in action.

I don't know if Josiah will become president—would there be an armored buggy? But I do know that the Grange needs to be a place where people feel at home. When we look at our traditions and our heritage, we have

much to help us encourage that. We just have to figure
out how to marry tradition and today instead of forcing
them to collide.

Defining Relevance

Well, for those who are regular readers, I will share that I finished the book *Josiah for President.* Since I don't want to spoil it for those who might want to read it, I'll say that it's arguable whether or not it ended well—but there were some interesting twists and turns. As noted last month, it did raise some questions worthy of consideration by Grangers.

Many thanks to those who posted positive comments on last month's column, especially Mary Doherty who wrote, "Thanks for this message. I sometimes have difficulty explaining the Grange's relevance in this fast-paced society. This helps."

Can an Amishman serve as President? Is the Grange still relevant? Those are good, important questions. Where do we find the answers?

We find the answers to the second question inside our Granges and inside ourselves.

In my role as communications director, I communicate with lots of people both inside and outside the Grange. Too often, I hear "We're probably going to have to close… haven't had a meeting for months… can't get a quorum." The reasons given are many. But I think it ultimately comes down to a question of relevance.

Let me defend that point by sharing that I also spoke with a Granger today who reported that her Grange is "adding new members at every meeting." When she talks excitedly about those new members, I hear the relevance that Grange has in its community. Those new members are seeing that Grange as relevant to their lives and work. Yet another Grange shared the news of a new member family thanks to their search for a place to hold their wedding reception. When the bride visited the hall, she was impressed with the friendliness and work of that

Grange and decided to become part of it.

These are modern-day examples of the lesson of history. The Grange didn't come into being because the founders thought it would be a good idea to create a fraternal organization and perform a ritual. The Grange came into being because there was a need—a need to organize farmers, to create community, and to *"labor together for the common good."*

For many communities (and their resident Granges) that need (opportunity, really) is resurfacing today. I chuckled with the master of another exciting local Grange who said "We're doing it by going 'retro.'" In this case, retro means relevance. The purpose the Grange served for farmers years ago is becoming necessary. This Grange has discovered a local opportunity to organize farmers, create community, and "labor together for the common good."

On a different front, Valley Grange recently hosted a Project Linus event, calling for "Blanketeers" who were willing to put their hands to a simple task and make blankets for kids who would benefit from some comfort. The fact it was scheduled around the time of some tragic events involving kids made it even more relevant. We had lots of people show up—including several women who drove at least thirty miles to both see if they could help and see what it would take to do something similar in their area.

There's one other important component. This blanket-making was actually organized by a high school student named Heather Burgess. She's got passion and she wants to make a difference in children's lives. How can a Grange not support that? More importantly, if we are supporting things like this how can we not be relevant?

My explanation to the reporter who covered this event was, "We love to see people come together and do things for the benefit of the community, The Grange's history and heritage is all about supporting rural communities and these are the kinds of efforts that are meaningful."

There are some words that we should be hearing as we meander around the Grange Way of Life: "relevance, passion, meaningfulness."

As you sit through your next meeting listen carefully during the order of the business. When committee reports are called for if you are hearing "No report, Worthy Master," the odds are pretty good your Grange has a relevance problem. Perhaps under "new business" there's an opportunity to discuss passion and meaning. When I picture those Grange meetings from our early years, I don't hear "no report." I hear the excitement, friendship, perhaps even healthy debate. Why? Because the "Grange Way of Life" was owned by those who belonged. It was more accurately a case of "This is our way of life and our Grange supports it."

I remember being at a Grange meeting a few years ago. A young couple arrived with their children—I introduced myself, talked to the kids and assumed they were members because they seemed comfortable and fit right in. In time, they admitted it was their first time attending. It was almost an apology. They described the life they were trying to create for their family and said, "We heard this is the place we have to be if we want help doing that. We wish we'd got here sooner."

That, my friends, is relevance.

Clean the Kitchen

"As we are again to separate and mingle with the world, let us not forget the principles of our order. Let us add dignity to labor, and in our dealings with our fellow men, be honest, be just, and fear not. We must avoid intemperance in eating, drinking, and language, also in work and recreation, and whatever we do, strive to do well. Let us be quiet, peaceful citizens, feeding the hungry, helping the fatherless and widows, and keeping ourselves unspotted from the world."

If you recognized that as the master's charge before closing the Grange and skipped over it quickly, let me encourage you to go back and re-read thoughtfully. It is a nice little summary of the Grange Way of Life.

Elections are right around the corner. As we contemplate who will be the leaders of our Grange, let us not forget the jobs they are challenged with. Not only is it important they exemplify the Grange Way of Life, they should be leading us in the real work and value our Granges are providing.

With the help of a blog post recently written by Seth Godin, I'd like to suggest some of the perhaps "non-traditional" things a Grange Leader should do. For that matter, they might apply to every member:

- Add energy to every conversation
- Treat people better than they expect
- Offer help to others before it is asked for
- Highlight the good work that others do
- Get smarter by reading and learning
- Encourage curiosity
- Figure out what doesn't work and change it

- Do the unexpected occasionally

- Find people to join the team (membership comes later)

- Tackle the tough decisions

- Allow occasional silliness

- Organize the kitchen

- Clean something

- Start something

- Tell a joke at no one's expense

- Smile a lot

Within the framework of the principles of our order, we can expand the master's charge and perhaps give it more meaning as we work together in our Granges and as we "mingle with the world." Be honest, be just, fear not, and smile a lot!

Time to Stop Hiding?

Most Grangers who've heard the Ritual repeatedly will report having a favorite passage or two. While I find mine change and shift, this is a favorite time of year because I look forward to hearing one very important truth during the opening of the Installation of officers.

"The Order of the Patrons of Husbandry is the only association whose teachings accompany its members in their daily pursuits. They form part of the farmer's life. They do not call him from his work to put his mind upon any other subject but furnish recreation in his daily duties, and, by cheerful instruction lighten and elevate his labor."

That deserves some exploration. We are hearing and saying "that's the Grange Way" a lot this year, thanks to National Grange adopting it as a slogan or motto. But what, exactly is the Grange Way?

While it might be challenging to describe it in 500 words or less, I know where to find the answer–it lies in the what we call the Ritual or, perhaps more accurately, the teachings of the Grange. Personally, I think there is really no one "Grange Way." There are different Grange Ways that are linked together and have much in common. Perhaps the question is as important as the answer. My personal favorite answer is found in the Grange Motto. The Grange Way is: in essentials, unity; in non-essentials, freedom; in all things charity.

But when I think about "The Grange Way" and its many meanings, I'm led to two disturbing conclusions about our Order.

First, too often our teachings are neglected and we lose the connections between our teachings and our daily life. "Grange" becomes a place we go once a month. And while there, too often we simply go through the motions, a very real hazard found when practicing the Ritual and maintaining tradition. Perhaps we need reminding of why we "go to Grange" so our daily labor is lightened and elevated.

I occasionally scare traditionalists by departing from the Ritual—or more accurately, interrupting the language and flow of the Ritual. For the good of the order, I want to know what we are doing as individuals and a Grange to "nurture hope?" We pledge to do that at least twice in every meeting, seems like we ought to give some thought to how we follow through. The Grange is about life; it is not merely about meetings.

My second concern closely relates to the first. I haven't counted, but I think most Grangers would agree education and instruction are mentioned repeatedly throughout all of the Ritual. Does our practice reflect that? Hosting a workshop about seed starting counts, but does every meeting we attend leave us challenged and energized? Are we exploring our traditions and the Grange Way of Life?

One Grange I have spoken with is considering spreading the degrees over an extended period of time. Why? Because they think it would be great to have some discussion among new and experienced members after each degree to explore what the candidates have learned while reminding others of Grange Teaching. I think that's awesome. We know it is time to deemphasize the secret aspects of the order. Yes, they did serve a positive purpose years ago but it's time to come out from behind the password and secret work. We need to leave our halls to stand in our community next to our neighbors and friends. The Grange Way has a lot to offer. We have to discover the big opportunity to talk about that openly in ways that are exciting and relevant. Maybe it starts with, *"The Grange and its teachings will accompany you in your daily pursuits..."*

If we truly want to be relevant in today's society, it's time to follow our own teachings and discover how those teachings contribute to our daily lives. I am not a fan of elevator speeches because they become contrived. When I coach people to work with the media, we learn "sound bites." Those are simple nuggets, ideally delivered in ten to fifteen seconds. The reporter is hoping to hear passion and spontaneity, not a canned speech. There may be millions of people, glued to their TVs, waiting for your answer. You've got fifteen seconds to tell them,

What is "the Grange Way?"

Is the Grange a Fraternity?

We stopped by a small school with some dictionaries… when the teacher heard we were there he asked us to come in and spend some time with the kids. Normally we conduct a fairly formal presentation with props that include a mailbox and staves. This time I had to "wing it."

After explaining a bit about the Grange and a few basic dictionary skills, I decided to have a few "dictionary races." (The kids hold up their dictionaries, I write a word on the board, and we see who can find the word first.) Normally we do a few words and stop. Not these kids.

I swear they would have played all day. And the teacher made it clear I should keep going—it was the end of the year and he wanted the kids to have some fun.

We'd been through all the words I usually use—patron, husbandry, etc. that can be used to explain the Grange. I was trying to come up with another when the teacher interjected, "Boys and girls, remember this morning when I told you the Grange would be coming? Remember I explained that it was a **fraternity**? Let's look that up!"

There wasn't time to consider his word choice. "Ready, set, go!"

But there is now. With the help of the Internet, I've poked around and found he might have been closer to right than I originally thought. We tend to associate, somewhat accurately, fraternities with colleges. Anybody ever consider a Grange Hall as our "frat house?" According to CNN, there are about 800,000 college students who currently belong to a fraternity or sorority. And while we connotatively associate fraternities with hazing, drinking, and partying, many of those fraternities "give back to their communities through volunteer work and rely on their network of brothers and sisters for lifelong friendships and professional connections."

However, the media has of late paid more attention to the negative aspects of fraternities, noting, for example, that there were four fraternity pledge-related deaths last year.

As far as I know, we've not had any deaths during degree work and Obligation Ceremonies. Obviously, I am having some fun with this but there are some interesting comparisons. One of the articles I read was written in an attempt to help freshmen decide whether or not to join a fraternity. It is also interesting that some statistics suggest fraternity and sorority membership is growing.

Among the definitions of "fraternity" are "a group of people sharing a common profession or interests" and "the state or feeling of friendship and mutual support within a group." A fraternity may often be a GLO (Greek Letter Organization) based on Greek Life.

Could we (should we?) think of the Grange as a fraternity based on rural life? It is an interesting question.

One of the recommendations for college students considering a fraternity is, in general terms, a warning that the fraternity actually may become too important and powerful, requiring submission. (Hazing is just one example.) A fraternity can be insulating and isolating and may even require a member to tolerate or support behavior they might not otherwise.

As I ponder all this I find myself remembering that our founders did not create a fraternal organization (or fraternity) to support farmers. They kept the proverbial cart behind the horse. Purpose came first. The fraternity is a by-product—an important byproduct, but nevertheless secondary to the purpose.

I believe the growth of college fraternities is attributable to a number of factors, but the important one is purpose. As I have written here before, our Granges struggle when there is no purpose. Simply getting together to enjoy a feeling of friendship and connection isn't enough to create the energy and excitement necessary for growth. I had an interesting conversation several years ago with someone who believed the Grange should be open to everyone. It's a lofty but impractical ideal. When we study the teachings, declaration of principles, etc. it should become apparent the Grange is not for everyone. When we fail to realize that and effectively say "anyone can be a member" we defeat our purpose and we defeat ourselves.

Prior to that day with those kids and their teacher, I would not have considered the Grange a fraternity. One of the things I highly value about the Grange is that it provides teaching and learning both in practice and in daily life. I've occasionally told people that one of the values of becoming a Granger is "it will make you think." Tradition and the Ritual are comforting and do create "a feeling of friendship and mutual support." The hazard that accompanies tradition and the Ritual is a tendency to stop thinking.

The founders tried to strike a balance between being comfortable and being challenged. Let's not lose that balance. The Grange Way of life is not just tradition and the Ritual, it's also about thinking and moving in the direction of our true purpose.

What Do We Do at a Grange Meeting?

This was actually a column about communication, but it's also about Grange Life. I include it because it raises the question of how others see (and hear) us.

As luck would have it, we sat near the restrooms during a recent restaurant visit. At one point a young fellow came across the room, clearly on a mission. When he arrived at the doors he stopped short and I watched his head swivel from door to door. I sensed the problem and his anxiety.

I hopped up, walked over and used my finger to underline the word "men" in "gentlemen," noting that I was quite sure that was the door he was looking for. He was in a bit of a rush and said nothing, but I sensed his relief and appreciation.

Now I'm quite sure whoever made and hung that sign didn't consider the possibility that some young lad wouldn't recognize the word "gentlemen." Or perhaps the sign-maker assumed a child with a limited reading vocabulary wouldn't attempt to use the restroom unaccompanied. But for those of us interested in communication, we really ought to be more thoughtful. We tend to get so focused on what's in our heads, we don't consider what is (or isn't) in the heads of the people we are trying to communicate with.

I made the classic Maine mistake when my sister and her family visited recently. Without thinking, while giving them directions I said, "You're going to turn left where the schoolhouse used to be." My brother-in-law reminded me this was their first trip to Maine and that wasn't a particularly helpful instruction.

One of the many reasons I like hanging around with kids is they are great reminders of the need to choose words thoughtfully. Kids are very literal, and they haven't developed the filters adults have. Sometimes the misunderstandings can be funny. Many have heard my story about the time I accidentally used the word "deputy" when talking about the Grange to some third graders. This raised lots of questions about badges and guns.

What about adults? Our vocabulary is bigger and we have, hopefully, developed an ability to filter conversations. But we still face the same challenges—maybe even more.

Not long ago I had some dialog with a reporter who had "heard" some things about the Grange and wanted more information. As I listened to him, I could understand why he'd heard what he did, but while based on some basic truth it wasn't accurate. Fortunately, most reporters are instinctively curious and learn early in their careers to question, probe, and confirm. But another person might well have been satisfied with what they heard. They might also have passed along the incorrect perception.

Our restroom visitor teaches us the importance of thinking about what we say and write. Our reporter teaches us the importance of making certain we are hearing and reading correctly. Both the speaker and the listener do have responsibilities during a dialog.

We have an added challenge that I call "Grange Talk." Not unlike most organizations, we have a large vocabulary of words and expressions that are unfamiliar to many. Even our historical officer titles are unique. We know what a "master" is but others may wonder if we are his slaves—one reason there has been a trend to substitute the word president. I may hold the office of lecturer at Valley Grange, but when talking to non-Grangers I explain that I am the program director.

Imagine, if you can, talking with someone who knows absolutely nothing about the Grange. (There are many more than you might think.) If you start talking to him or her about floorwork and the Ritual, what impression are you giving? Think about the effect you are trying to create when you communicate. Choose words that your listener or reader uses. Go for precision. And try to include what are called "sensory" words that make your reader or listener feel something.

So now tell me, what do we do at a Grange Meeting?

How Much Can We Learn?

"You are now about to enter the harvest. God loveth a cheerful giver and no less a cheerful worker; for work is prayer." These words are part of the overseer's message to Fourth Degree Candidates. As Pomona Overseer, I occasionally have the honor of delivering that challenge. It contains many important messages but let's just look at one or two.

"Work is prayer." Prayer is communication. Think about that. I think those who authored this challenge hoped that the candidates wouldn't miss the application—it is a thread through the entire message. In the simplest form, work is prayer, prayer is communication, therefore work is communication. The work we do and the way we do it communicates.

The very next lines are *"Labor with cheerfulness. A merry heart doeth good like a medicine."* Think about <u>that</u>!

Most Grangers I talk with will admit remembering very little from their first exposure to the degrees. There are reasons for that, including the amount of instruction that's included at once. As an educator, I would say the designers of the Ritual did some really good stuff. They used examples and comparisons, repetition and techniques that kept the learners (candidates) engaged in the process. But I think they also counted on something that is, unfortunately, less true today than then.

Consider how often degree days were held during the Grange's explosive growth. I can only guess, but I don't think it would be unreasonable to think the degrees were offered at least quarterly and perhaps even monthly. The number isn't really important. What's important is the fact that a Granger "heard" the degrees often—certainly more than once!

Thus, Grangers had real opportunities to absorb the many messages and lessons. When I was preparing for this month's column I actually saw those important three words in a way I hadn't previously. "Work is prayer." It may take a second to say them. Less to read them. But how long could we spend considering their importance and application?

Work is prayer. Work with cheerfulness.

"A merry heart doeth good like a medicine." Medicine for whom? When you look at the Grange Way of Life in total, the answer is clear. Cheerful labor and a merry heart is good for others, good for our communities, and good for ourselves. That may be why the overseer continues for a bit on the point.

"The truest balsam for injured minds is cheerful labor." In today's language that states the value of having a purpose. In the extreme, how many of our mental health issues have at their roots a lack of purpose and connectivity? There is a story told about someone being hired at a good rate of pay. The job was to hit a log with the back side of an ax. Attracted to the potential pay, he began whacking at the log with the blunt side of the ax but quit after a relatively short period of time. When his employer asked him why he replied: "I have to see the chips fly." We, as individuals, and our work need a purpose. Work is prayer. Prayer is communication. Cheerful work has a purpose, keeps our minds healthy, and communicates to those around us.

The paragraph ends with, *"Cultivate the habit of looking for better and brighter days, instead of mourning over the past."* I like the use of the word "cultivate" here. I think it was used quite intentionally because farmers know what it means to cultivate. Looking for better and brighter days is not something you do once. Cheerful, purposeful work is one of the tools that helps us find better and brighter days.

Let me note that this is one paragraph from one lesson out of four degrees. Four sentences. Less than sixty words. At best a fleeting moment for candidate experiencing the degrees. How much can we learn by studying our traditions and the Ritual?

The Grange Mission

Mission Statements have, it seems, become a bit passé. That's unfortunate because a good mission statement is a big component in keeping organizations healthy and on point.

I recall once listening to a speaker who suggested families consider having a mission statement—a brief statement of the family's purpose. His does, and he claims that it helps them on a daily basis in many ways including decision-making and prioritizing.

The Grange Mission Statement is a bit lengthy— generally accepted practice suggests brevity is the soul of wit. But the good news is it gives us plenty to think about as individuals and an organization.

> *The Grange in the 21st Century will be a preeminent organization.*
>
> *It will commit to the development of the potential in families, youth and adults of all ages through dynamic programs and experiences that educate, engage and enrich lives.*
>
> *The Grange will be noted for its commitment to the membership through its enabled leadership, its financial and organizational strength, and its ability to make a difference in the lives of children, youth, families and individuals.*
>
> *The Grange will be a relevant, caring and involved part of the community in which its members are located. It will be well known and understood and considered a viable, involved and distinctive organization.*
>
> *A person who becomes a member can expect to find in the organization a clear and impressive pathway to membership, outstanding fellowship*

with leaders and respected citizens of the community, the encouragement to meet and make new friends and the opportunity to lead and be well led.

At the state and national level, the Grange will be flexible, well governed, proactive partner in support of issues that are relevant to members and the communities in which they live. It will be accountable to and supportive of the leadership and membership at the local Grange. The Grange will be responsive to the member's time, committed to membership growth, and designed for relevance and national preeminence.

Appendix A

Grange Declaration of Purposes

The Grange Declaration of Purposes is included here because it does help us understand the Grange Way of Life.

Preamble

Profoundly impressed with the truth that the National Grange of the Order of Patrons of Husbandry should proclaim to the world its general objectives, we hereby unanimously make this Declaration of Purposes.

General Objectives

United by the strong and faithful tie of an agricultural fraternity, yet welcoming all of good moral character to membership, we mutually resolve to labor for the good of our Order, our country, and mankind.

We heartily endorse the motto, "In essentials, unity; in non-essentials, liberty; in all things, charity."

Specific Objectives

We shall endeavor to advance our cause by striving to accomplish the following objectives:

- To develop a better and higher manhood and womanhood among ourselves; to enhance the comforts and attractions of our homes; to strengthen our attachments to our pursuits; to foster mutual understanding and cooperation; to maintain inviolate our laws, and to emulate each other in labor, in order to hasten the good time coming.

- We propose meeting together, talking together, working together, and in general, acting together for our mutual protection and advancement. We shall constantly strive to secure harmony, good will, and brotherhood, and to make our Order perpetual. We shall earnestly endeavor to suppress personal, local, sectional, and national prejudices, all unhealthy rivalry and all selfish ambition. Faithful adherence to these principles will insure our mental, moral, social and material advancement.

Business Relations

For our business interests we desire to bring producer and consumer into the most direct and friendly relations possible, remembering that "individual happiness depends upon general prosperity."

We are opposed to such spirit and management of any corporation or enterprise which tends to oppress people. We long to see the antagonism between capital and labor removed by common consent, and by statesmanship worthy of an enlightened people.

We are opposed to wages and salaries that exceed productive efficiency. We recommend that farmers buy wisely and produce efficiently to make their farms profitable; to make maximum use of the innovations of science and technology; to systematize their work and to calculate intelligently on probabilities.

To all we recommend sound money management that we may avoid insolvency and bankruptcy.

Education

We shall advance the cause of education by all just means within our power.

Influenced by our strong beliefs in the institution of the family, we are convinced that education begins in the family circle. Discipline is an essential part of education. Self-discipline comes with maturity. Until such time as this level of competency is reached, families and schools have a responsibility for enforcing adequate discipline.

We recognize the necessity of experimentation to develop new and better methods of education, but we caution against the widespread adoption of these innovative and experimental methods until they have been proven effective.

We recognize that education is a continuing process. We encourage all to continue their education through adult education classes, by continued reading, observation and such other methods as may be available, including radio, television and the internet.

We recognize the valuable contribution made to education by the printed word, especially in newspapers, periodicals and books, and will continue to advocate their widespread availability.

Outside Cooperation

Our Fraternity, being agriculturally based, family oriented and dedicated to the pure principles of equality under Constitutional Law, we appeal to all good citizens for mutual cooperation and assistance toward reform that we may remove from our midst the last vestige of inequity and corruption. We believe that harmony, equitable compromise and earnest cooperation are essential to future success.

The Grange—Not Partisan

We emphatically and sincerely assert the oft-repeated truth taught in our Constitutional Law, that the Grange—National, State, Pomona, or Subordinate—is not a partisan or party organization.

The principles we teach underlie all true statesmanship, and if properly carried out, will tend to purify the whole political atmosphere of our country; for we seek the greatest good to the greatest number.

We must always bear in mind that no one, by becoming a Patron of Husbandry, gives up that inalienable right and duty which belongs to every American citizen, to take a proper interest in the politics of one's country.

On the contrary, it is right for every member to do all in his or her power, legitimately, to influence for good the action of any political party to which he or she belongs. It is reserved by every Patron, as the right of a free citizen to affiliate with any party that will best carry out his or her principles.

We acknowledge the broad principle that difference of opinion is no crime, and hold that "progress toward truth is made by differences of opinion," while "the fault lies in bitterness of controversy."

We desire a proper equality, and fairness; protection for the weak; restraint upon the strong; in short, justly distributed power. These are American ideals, the very essence of American independence, and to advocate the contrary is unworthy of the sons and daughters of our Republic.

We cherish the belief that sectionalism is, and of right should be, dead and buried with the past. Our work is for the present and the future. In our agricultural fraternity we shall recognize no North, no South, no East, no West.

Conclusion

It shall be an abiding principle with us to relieve any of our oppressed and suffering members by any reasonable means at our command. We proclaim it among our purposes to continue our historical appreciation of the abilities and equality of women.

Imploring the continued assistance of our Divine Master to guide us in our work, we pledge ourselves to faithful and harmonious labor for all future time; to advance by our united efforts, to the wisdom, justice, fraternity and political purity so earnestly sought by the wise and courageous men and women who founded our noble Order.

Appendix B

About the Dictionary Project

Since the Dictionary Project (also known as "Words for Thirds" in the Grange) has been mentioned several times throughout the book, it seemed appropriate to include some additional information about it.

I've always enjoyed kids, but my experience with the Dictionary Project set me on a path that quite literally changed my life. Handing out dictionaries to third graders led me to discover a passion. It therefore seems appropriate to dedicate a few pages to this worthy cause.

The idea for The Dictionary Project began in 1992 when Annie Plummer of Savannah, Georgia, gave 50 dictionaries to children who attended a school close to her home. Each year she continued to give this gift, raising money to help give more and more books so that in her lifetime she raised enough money to buy 17,000 dictionaries for children in Savannah.

Early on, her project attracted the attention of Bonnie Beeferman of Hilton Head, S.C., who began a project of raising money by selling crafts to buy dictionaries for the schoolchildren of Hilton Head and the surrounding communities. By 1995, Bonnie was getting so many requests from local teachers to be included in the project that she wrote a letter to the editor of the Charleston Post and Courier explaining the project and asking for someone to help meet requests from the Charleston area.

Mary French, who was already an active school volunteer even though her two children were still of preschool age, read the letter and decided this was a project for her. Starting with a few schools in Charleston and Summerville, she realized quickly that providing dictionaries to all the students in Charleston was going to require serious fundraising. She and her late husband Arno French formed a 501(c)(3) nonprofit Association in 1995, along with a Board of Directors. Arno served as president, Mary became the director of the Association, and The Dictionary Project was born.

The program has been adopted and refined by individuals, businesses, and civic organizations all over the country. Groups such as Rotary Clubs, Kiwanis Clubs, Elks Lodges, Granges, Lions Clubs, The Republican Federation of Women, Pioneer volunteers, parent organizations, and many more, have implemented The Dictionary Project where they live. Anyone can participate in this project by sponsoring a program to provide dictionaries to children in their community. The dictionaries are a gift for the children to keep. Sponsors give dictionaries and other reference books to children in all 50 states and the District of Columbia, the Virgin Islands, Puerto Rico, 9 Canadian provinces, and more than 15 other countries around the world.

My personal experience with the project began when I was "elected" to represent the Grange by presenting dictionaries to the third graders at our local elementary school. I headed for school with the load of books and a sense of dread—expecting the kids to be bored and unappreciative of something so simple.

I left school that day feeling a lot differently. I'd grossly underestimated the power of words and how kids would respond. They were like little sponges, soaking up new information. I lost control of the presentation when they received their books. How could I compete with over all those new words?

The kids taught me a powerful lesson that day. And I'm pleased that over a decade later I am still learning from them.

Valley Grange of Guilford has expanded their program to now include four districts and five schools. Several of those schools make a "Dictionary Day Field Trip" to the Valley Grange Hall where they learn about the Grange, their dictionaries and how to use them, and what it means to be a steward.

There's a lot to like about this program, including how easy and affordable it is to support our kids on a very personal level. For additional information:

http://www.dictionaryproject.org

The Dictionary Project

P. O. Box 1845
Charleston, SC 29402
(843) 388-8375
(843) 856-2706

Appendix C

Bibliography and References

Boomsma, W. (2013). *Small People--Big Brains*. Abbot ME: Abbot
    Village Press.
Boomsma, W. (2015-2018). Retrieved from Abbot Village Press:
    wboomsma.com
Bye, Bye Longjohns. (2015). *Maine Policy Review, 24*(1).
Declaration of Purposes. (n.d.). Retrieved from National Grange:
        https://www.nationalgrange.org/
Exploring Traditions--Meandering Around the Grange Way of Life.
    (2014-2018). Retrieved from Maine State Grange:
    http://mainestategrange.org/
Gardener, C. M. (1949). *The Grange--Friend of the Farmer*. Washington
    DC: National Grange of the Patrons of Husbandry.
Godin, S. (2017, 2018). Retrieved from Seth's Blog:
    https://seths.blog/
Grosh, R. A. (1876). *Mentor in the Granges and Homes of Patrons of
    Husbandry*. New York, NY: Clark & Maynard.
Howe, S. R. (1994). A Fair Field and No Favor. In S. R. Howe, *A Fair
    Field and No Favor*. Augusta Maine: Maine State Grange.
Manual of Pomona Granges (Thirteenth ed.). (1997). Washington, DC:
    National Grange, Patrons of Husbandry.
Manual of Subordinate Granges (Forty-sixth ed.). (2013). Washington,
    DC: National Grange, Patrons of Husbandry.
The Grange Songbook. (1983). Washington DC: The National Grange.
Wilson, P. L. (2003). *Grange Appeal*. Retrieved 2018, from The
    Anarchist Library:
    https://theanarchistlibrary.org/library/peter-lamborn-
    wilson-grange-appeal

About the Author

Walter Boomsma is the author of "Small People—Big Brains: Stories About Simplicity, Exploration, and Wonder." He has served as Communications Director for the Maine State Grange since 2014 and has been a member of Valley Grange in Guilford Maine since 2003.

In 2015, he began writing a monthly column for the Maine State Grange website designed to explore some of the rich tradition and history of the Grange. Several of those columns have been reprinted in *Good Day!*™, the magazine of the National Grange.

In addition to a published author, he is an educator of adults and a substitute elementary school teacher. He is an active proponent of good mental health and a NAMI certified Mental Health First Aid Specialist for youth and adults.

He and his wife Janice make their home in Abbot Maine.

Walter is available to speak at your live event. For information or to book an event, contact him at 207 343-1842 or visit WBoomsma.com

About Small People—Big Brains

In "Small People – Big Brains" the author shares some of his experiences with kids as a volunteer and, most recently, substitute elementary school teacher. Many of these short stories will make you laugh. Some will make you cry. All will make you think.

In the pages of this "collection of stories about simplicity, exploration, and wonder," you'll meet a second grader who becomes quite certain Mr. Boomsma is ignorant of the basic facts of life. How the young student handles this delicate situation is a lesson in tact that many adults should learn.

You'll also encounter a nine-year-old who thinks he's "an excellent reader and extremely smart" until he's forced to consider that being smart is about knowing what he doesn't know.

The title of the book comes from an encounter with a young fellow who was firmly convinced that his difficulties at school were the result of his brain being too small. The stories, however, prove that these small people really do have big brains. They just haven't discovered and fully learned how to use them yet.

The author shares his first story in the preface. It's about fourth graders reading a story together until the teacher stopped them and asked them to guess the ending. (The story was about a mouse that was unhappy that he was receiving less attention since the birth of his baby brother.) The students were sharing their guesses and one fellow suggested either the mouse or his brother might disappear thanks to the family cat. His classmate used that you've-got-to-be-kidding tone when she said, "It's a children's book! I doubt that anyone's going to get eaten."

While this isn't a children's book, no one gets eaten. But the author's hope for you is that you do get entertained and challenged. He's also betting by the end of the book you'll find your brain is bigger than you realized.

Small People—Big Brains is available from Amazon in both print and Kindle versions.

"This is a light, fast read until it isn't, and then you stop and read a sentence or a thought a couple of times… A light touch and some solid content is what you will see and what 'Mr. Boomsma' hopes you get…"

Jack Falvey, frequent contributor to
The Wall Street Journal and Barron's

Books by Abbot Village Press

Small People—Big Brains
Stories About Simplicity, Exploration, and Wonder

By Mr. Boomsma

ISBN-10: 1482033070
ISBN-13: 978-1482033076

Maine Real Estate Law and Rule Handbook

Edited by Walter Boomsma

ISBN-10: 1494319446
ISBN-13: 978-1494319441

Abbot Historical Society Calendar Photo Book
People and Places Around Abbot Maine

Edited by Walter Boomsma

ISBN-10: 1979648875
ISBN-13: 978-1979648875

Exploring Traditions—
Celebrating the Grange Way of Life

By Walter Boomsma

ISBN-10: 172590537X
ISBN-13: 978-1725905375

Abbot Village Press publications are available on Amazon.com and Barnes and Noble and our online store at http://wboomsma.com..

Abbot Village Press also publishes the *Piscataquis Community Elementary School Yearbook*, available for private (in-school) sale only.

Abbot Village Press
Books, Blogs & Education with purpose

17 River Road

Abbot ME 04406

www.ingramcontent.com/pod-product-compliance
Lightning Source LLC
Chambersburg PA
CBHW051103250726
48656CB00001B/454

9 781725 905375